To my god
Gen. Wayne "Speedie" and
Nancy Lloyd.
Best wishes,
J. Kemp McLaughlin
10 Sept. 2000

The Mighty Eighth in WWII

The Mighty Eighth in WWII

A Memoir

Brig. Gen. J. Kemp McLaughlin
USAFR (Ret.)

THE UNIVERSITY PRESS OF KENTUCKY

Scholarly publisher for the Commonwealth,
serving Bellarmine College, Berea College, Centre
College of Kentucky, Eastern Kentucky University,
The Filson Club Historical Society, Georgetown College,
Kentucky Historical Society, Kentucky State University,
Morehead State University, Murray State University,
Northern Kentucky University, Transylvania University,
University of Kentucky, University of Louisville,
and Western Kentucky University.
All rights reserved.

Editorial and Sales Offices: The University Press of Kentucky
663 South Limestone Street, Lexington, Kentucky 40508-4008

04 03 02 01 00   5 4 3 2 1

Frontispiece: The author and crew ready to lead the 1st Air Division on a
raid in September 1943. *Front, left to right,* Lt. Ed T. O'Grady, bombardier,
F/O Tim Eaton, navigator, Capt. Henry A. Hughes, navigator, Col. William
M. Reid, air commander, S/Sgt. Foley. *Back, left to right,* Lt. Young S/Sgt.
Brubaker, S/Sgt. Ford, S/Sgt. Van Horn, T/Sgt. Edison, Capt. Kemp
McLaughlin.(U.S. Army Air Corps photo)

Library of Congress Cataloging-in-Publication Data

McLaughlin, J. Kemp, 1918–
    The mighty Eighth in WWII : a memoir / J. Kemp McLaughlin.
      p. cm.
    Includes index.
    ISBN 0-8131-2178-7 (alk. paper)
    1. United States. Army Air Forces. Air Force, 8th.—History, 2. World
War, 1939–1945—Aerial operations, American. 3. McLaughlin, J. Kemp,
1918– . 4. World War, 1939–1945—Personal narratives, American.
5. United States. Army Air Forces. Air Force, 8th—Biogoraphy. I. Title:
Mighty 8th in World War Two. II. Title: Mighty 8th in World War 2.
III. Title.
D790.M434   2000
940.54'4973'092—dc21   00-028305
[B]

This book is dedicated to Hugh Edward McLaughlin, who helped defeat Chief Cornstalk at the Battle of Point Pleasant, the opening battle of the American Revolution, and who fought with the "Men of Augusta" throughout that war. And to James Buchanan McLaughlin, Company C, 25th Virginia Infantry, C.S.A., who fought so valiantly with Stonewall Jackson and later with Robert E. Lee. And lastly to Elizabeth Harlow McLaughlin and James Blaine McLaughlin II, who I hope will never have to endure another war.

Contents

Preface   ix

1. Baptism   1

2. In the Beginning   8

3. Off We Go   18

4. Torch   27

5. Err'n in Erin   42

6. 1943   52

7. Pete's Story   67

8. Schweinfurt and Stuttgart   79

9. Assembling "The Mighty Eighth"   90

10. Schweinfurt Again   97

11. A New Base and My Longest Day   112

12. Group Operations   120

13. Escape and Evasion   124

14. 1944   150

15. Headquarters   158

16. D-Day and the Fall Campaign   172

17. Aerial Operations   181

18. My War's End   187

19. A Look Back   194

Afterword   197

Appendix   198

Index   201

Illustrations follow page 118

Preface

World War II was by far the greatest event to have occurred in the twentieth century. Its great battles, in the air, on the ground, at sea, were felt in every nation and by nearly every living person. And so it was with me.

In 1941, I was a twenty-two-year-old college student, facing the draft and an almost certain war. Having earned a pilot's license, I elected to try for the then budding U.S. Army Air Corps, for flying was great fun and the most appealing thing I had ever experienced.

This is the story of the events and the air combat that ensued from my enlistment in 1941 until my discharge from service in 1946. It is also my tale of some great and brave Americans who were my friends and comrades in arms in the European and the North African Theaters of Operations. The reader should bear in mind that much of what is related here is from memories of events of more than fifty years ago, and some dates, names, and times of events may be in error.

In trying to recall the specifics of events of a half century ago that comprise this narrative, I found myself turning at times to my friends and associates from the United States 8th Air Force and especially those of the 92nd Bombardment Group. I wish to thank Col. David Alford of Rising Star, Texas, William P. Edris of Kernersville, North Carolina, and Jack Spratt of Toledo, Ohio. Also John S. Sloan, to whose diary of the 92nd Bombardment Group I have referenced many times for facts and figures that I never could have obtained elsewhere. I also wish to thank Lt. Col. Lester Lennox, formerly of the 95th Bombardment Group, who wrote the book *Assembling the Mighty Eighth,* and who generously gave permission for its inclusion in the writing of my story. Additionally, I wish to thank Richard McKee for his encouragement and help in editing and bringing this book to fruition.

1

Baptism

It began on a cool October morning in 1942 at Bovingdon Aerodrome, Hertfordshire, England. It seemed strangely quiet as the realization began to descend on me that I was about to embark on my first combat mission of World War II.

Before we left the States for England in August 1942, Col. James Sutton, our group commander, had briefed us at length on his version of how the air campaign against Germany would be conducted. He told us our B-17Fs were invincible, that with their firepower and ability to fly at higher altitudes the German air force would be no match for us. And lastly, that we could expect to be back home in six to ten months. We, of course, believed him.

While we were still in Bangor, Maine, he prepared us for what would be the first nonstop group flight to England. The 97th and 301st Bomb Groups, one of whom we had trained with at MacDill Field in Florida, had flown the route in a series of hops, from Gander, Newfoundland, to Greenland, then to Iceland, and on to Scotland, in July 1942 and had lost several of their planes. These losses were due to a lack of pilot experience and to a minimum amount of instrument-flying instruction. And, with the erratic, difficult-to-forecast weather conditions in the North Atlantic, our group commander knew that the same fate could easily befall us. B-17s were in such short supply in those days that it was almost unconscionable to lose even one from lack of planning.

Colonel Sutton had received permission from Gen. Henry H. "Hap" Arnold, commander of United States Army Air Forces, for our group to fly directly from Gander to Prestwick, Scotland, and avoid the precarious approaches and landings in the fjords en route. We had equipped each B-17 with an additional five hundred gallons of fuel, or about twelve hours of flying time. The distance was approximately two thousand miles, and with a cruising speed of about 185 miles per hour, we could make it with enough fuel left to get to an alternate destination if necessary. Since we had all flown lengthy cruise-control flights before this ocean-crossing flight, we knew for certain that none of our ships was a fuel hog.

All thirty-six of our group's airplanes flew to Prestwick without mishap and with the loss of only one engine en route: Lt. Charles Austin, the only other pilot from my hometown of Charleston, West Virginia, lost an engine in mid-ocean. In order to keep up with his squadron, he began to lighten his airplane by tossing overboard nonessential supplies. After several radio exchanges with his commander, he was asked if he carried any whiskey onboard. He finally admitted he did and was ordered to toss it overboard. Reluctantly he told his crew to throw overboard nine cases of bourbon whiskey. 'Twas a sad affair, for there was not a drop of bourbon to be found in all of England. After our successful attempt, all of the groups flying to the European Theater would make the direct flight.

Our group had flown its first mission on September 6, 1942, to Meaulte, France, to bomb the Avions Potez aircraft factory. This raid took place exactly six months after the group had been activated on March 6, 1942 (making it the oldest group in the 8th Air Force). My squadron, the 407th Bomb Squadron, did not participate in this raid. Instead, we flew out into the English Channel as if we were en route to another target to the north, in an effort to lead as many German fighters as possible away from the main effort to Meaulte. (We got no combat credit for these diversionary flights.) The other three squadrons of the group, namely, the 325th Bomb Squadron, furnished fourteen B-17Es for this raid. They were heavily attacked by German fighters, and the 327th Bomb Squadron lost one ship and its crew, the first 8th Air Force loss of the air war in Europe. The 301st and the 97th Bomb Groups also participated in this raid with sixteen B-17s, losing one plane.

With this new air war experience fresh in my mind, I went with trepidation to my first mission briefing at 6 A.M. All air crews selected to participate gathered with their respective squadrons in our group operations briefing room. On stage was a large map of Europe with a piece of white yarn marking our route to the city of Lille in northern France. Our target would be the steel mills located there. Colonel Sutton gave us a short talk stressing the fact that this was to be the first 8th Air Force maximum effort and that a hundred B-17s would participate. (This would be the first raid of the war composed of one hundred or more B-17s.) Maj. Willie Buck, group operations officer, gave us the route information with station and en-route times for the various points along the way. He stated that the 325th Squadron would lead the group and that our squadron, the 407th, would be the high squadron and fly left and above the group leader.

We were to take off at 8 A.M., assemble over the airport at one thousand feet aboveground and then climb to twenty-five thousand feet (in formation), join the other groups at the English coast, and proceed to the target. Next, Maj. Gardiner Fiske, our chief intelligence officer, briefed us on expected enemy activity. Major Fiske was from a prominent Boston family and had been a member of the famous Lafayette Esquadrille in World War I. He had rushed back into service with little modern-day expertise for our mission. At the end of Major Fiske's briefing, someone asked him about antiaircraft guns along the French coast on our route. He looked puzzled and finally said, "Well, there weren't any there when I was there in World War I." Colonel Sutton jumped up and said, "Gordy, for God's sake, sit down!" An ironic but constrained laugh arose from the audience.

As I look back on that scene now, I realize that, sadly, no one in the Army Air Corps knew at that time how to utilize the B-17 or how to conduct the air war against the German military forces effectively. It was a learn-as-you-go affair.

We all arrived at our airplanes by 0800 hours and began our checks to make certain that everything was in place and ready. At 0840 hours we started our engines and began taxiing into position. I was assigned as copilot on my squadron commander (Maj. Bob Keck's) crew. We were leading our 407th Squadron. We taxied onto the take off runway with our wingmen following and the low 327th Squadron behind them. After crew checks and engine run-ups, we began our take off roll at 1000 hours. We formed up over the field and began our climb eastward along our planned route. We joined another group in trail at the coast at about fifteen thousand feet and continued our climb. It was a bright clear morning, and we were climbing directly into the sun when Major Keck decided we were closing too fast on the lead squadron.

Without notifying his wingmen, he reduced power, and they began to overrun his lead ship. As they fought to stay in formation and began to maneuver back and forth, Lt. Eugene Wiley's numbers three and four propellers chopped the vertical stabilizer entirely off Lt. Jimmy Dempsey's airplane. Both slipped out of formation and luckily made it back to England. Wiley landed with two good engines at a Royal Air Force field and Lieutenant Dempsey made it back to our home base at Bovingdon. Five other airplanes turned back because of mechanical failures. Here we learned the hard way that you could not climb heavily loaded bombers in formation for long periods without severely damaging the engine and propeller systems.

As we drew near the French coast at about twenty-four thousand feet, the group in front suddenly turned north, and we proceeded on alone. Inland, a thin layer of haze began to form, and though we could all clearly see the serene countryside directly below, it became very difficult to see at a forward angle, particularly with the bright sun directly in front of us. As we approached Lille, the bombardier could not see the target, so we began a right turn to our secondary target, the airfield at St. Omer. As we dropped our bombs, we ran into heavy and very accurate antiaircraft fire from 88mm guns. We saw pink and green flak bursts as well as black ones, probably signals to the enemy fighters or antiaircraft gunners to show them where their shots were going.

As we made a turn off the target, heading west toward the coast, we took a direct hit in the left wing, in the number two gas tank. A huge fire ensued, streaming well beyond the tail of our airplane. Simultaneously another near burst threw shrapnel through the center of the airplane, wounding the radio operator, who began screaming over the interphone, blocking all other communication. Our waist gunner, S/Sgt. Archie Cothren, expecting the ship to explode or go down, bailed out. Major Keck signaled me to take over and went below, I assumed to fight the fire. Our top turret gunner, who doubled as flight engineer, had gotten out of his turret to try to extinguish the fire. The rest of the group formation was pulling away from us because we had lost our number two engine and could not feather the propeller. Knowing that we could not survive the German fighters alone and crippled, I lowered the nose of the airplane to gain enough speed to stay under the group until we could reach the coast. The fighters were attacking from the rear, and the puffs of exploding 20mm shells were all around us. Suddenly the tail gunner came into the cockpit saying the fire was so hot he couldn't stay in his turret.

The next moment I looked out my right window and found myself face to face with a German fighter pilot in a Focke-Wulf 190. I'm sure he saw our fire and our waist gunner bail out, and with no one shooting back at him, he must have wondered why we didn't go down, so he came up to look in our cockpit. He then rolled out to the right and swung back to his left and began firing at us, but he hadn't allowed himself enough room, and I could see his tracers well ahead of the nose of our airplane. As he passed under us at a very close range our ball turret gunner nailed him. He pulled up into a steep left roll, his plane smoking heavily, and disappeared in a dive.

The fighter attacks ceased, and our wing fire had about burnt itself out. Soon we were crossing the French coast, homeward bound. The English Channel never looked so good. I had descended to nineteen thousand feet when one of the two navigators came into the cockpit and said, "For heaven's sake get down—we have no oxygen up front." (As lead ship, we carried two navigators to make certain we'd find our target.) I looked at my oxygen gauge, and it read empty. We had lost all of our oxygen when we were first hit, but my juices were doing double time and I'd never realized that we had no oxygen. I then descended to ten thousand feet and could see the English coast ahead when suddenly Major Keck climbed back up into the cockpit and sat down in the first-pilot's seat. I learned later from our navigators that when the aircraft caught fire he had climbed below, buckled up his chute, and sat on the lower escape hatch, thinking the airplane would blow up. Though it would take a year to catch up with him, that incident eventually ended his military career.

We successfully made it back to our base, always turning away from our bad engine, and landed safely—all of us totally wrung out from our first combat experience. The fire in our left wing left a hole about four feet by four feet completely through the wing, and the paint on the left side of the plane was burnt all the way back to the tail. We parked near Jimmy Dempsey's rudderless airplane and climbed out to a speechless group. Our radio operator was taken directly to the hospital and survived to fly another day.

After a brief interrogation by our intelligence section, I rode my bike back to my quarters and en route passed one of my flying school classmates headed toward group headquarters. He was staring straight ahead and never acknowledged me when I spoke. I later learned that he, too, had been on the Lille mission and was on his way to turn in his wings. He'd had enough and refused to fly again.

It had been a rough day. In addition to the loss of Archie Cothren, our waist gunner, the group had also lost Lt. Francis Chorak and his entire crew. They were shot down in flames five miles northwest of St. Omer. His copilot that day was Lt. Joe Fracchia, another flying school classmate, whom I would not see again until VJ Day in the Roosevelt Hotel in New Orleans. As a lieutenant colonel, I felt regret that my classmate had only been promoted to the grade of first lieutenant after spending two and a half years as a prisoner of war. S/Sgt. Archie Cothren became a prisoner of war, held in Germany until May 1945.

Group morale among the air crews began to hit an all-time low. We'd lost two crews and half a dozen airplanes were damaged, some beyond repair. These two raids began to separate the men from the boys, as several officers began to find positions that would take them out of combat. One became the 8th Air Force oxygen officer (I never knew what his duties were). Another went to the 8th Air Force Headquarters, and several became instructors or staff at the newly formed 1/11th Combat Crew Replacement Center, which Gen. Ira C. Eaker, commander of the 8th Air Force, had ordered our group to establish.

I'd had my initiation into World War II air combat and now began to realize that, with future sorties ranging deeper into the continent, our chances of survival were pretty slim. In fact it would take miracles to make it safely through the war.

2

In the Beginning

Halfway through college I felt as if I were spinning my wheels. I didn't know what I wanted to do in life, and I felt as if I was wasting my father's money in college. The Army Air Corps Testing Team arrived on the West Virginia University campus in April 1938, and I decided to give it a try. About two dozen of us took the tests, and six of us passed it. My upper classmate Joe Cummingham from Clarksburg, West Virginia, was one of them. He went directly into training in 1939, served in North Africa, and finished his career as a major general—as commander-in-chief of the Alaskan Command. I was enthusiastic and "raring to go" then also, but I wasn't twenty-one years of age yet, and my parents would not sign a required agreement for me. Eighteen months later I was again tested and received an appointment for the class of 42D, to begin training on September 3, 1941. In the meantime, I had completed the primary and advanced phases of the College Pilot Training Program being conducted at West Virginia University.

I was sworn in at Fort Hayes, Ohio, and told to complete several forms. One required the names of all organizations of which I was a member. I listed my college fraternity and a pseudo college fraternity, very popular at that time, known as the "Fi Batar Kappar." Its principle reason for being was to keep the freshman men in line and otherwise just raise hell. It became so rowdy after the war that it was thrown off campus. I mention it here only because of what it led to eight months later.

Along with the other inductees, I boarded the train that afternoon, the third of September 1941, for Maxwell Army Air Corps Field, Alabama. We arrived the following afternoon to be greeted by a bunch of Army Air Corps lieutenants, who immediately began hazing us as if we were college frosh, even though all of us were college graduates.

We spent the next four weeks learning to be soldiers, getting shots, cadet uniforms, and so forth. We were kept on the double all the time, and I laugh yet when I recall a Limey in a British unit next to my barracks. His unit had just been ordered to "fall in" in the rain early one morning, and I heard him say, "Is this the first screwing we get today?"

At Maxwell Field my commander was Capt. James Luper. He was a much feared officer, and little did I know that I would see him shot down over Merseberg, Germany, two years later. At the end of September our group was divided among three different flying schools, and I was sent to Canton, Mississippi, a small town twenty minutes north of Jackson on the road to Memphis. There we met our upper class (42C), and the hazing began all over again. One cadet was given half a commode seat and when asked why, he reported that he carried it for a picture frame for some of his half-assed upperclassmen. Each such retort usually earned him a few extra demerits.

The flying school was run by the Mississippi Institute of Aeronautics and owned by Parks Aviation of St. Louis. They had contracts for several such schools in the southeastern area of the United States. We were assigned to squadrons, each of which had its own tactical officer, a U.S. Army Air Corps lieutenant who reported to the Air Corps base commander, a senior captain at the time.

All of our flight instructors were civilians, and I unluckily was assigned along with five other cadets to Mr. Russell Kerr from Pittsburgh, Pennsylvania. At our first meeting with him he informed us that we would probably all be washed out by the next week, and he wanted us to know it then and not be caught by surprise. I later learned that he told each class the same. Sure enough, by the next week four had washed out and the fifth was told he was on thin ice. Having already learned to fly, I could execute well enough to get by and felt confident that I would pass.

My classmate who was about to wash out asked me to accompany him to the commander's office to appeal his case and get a new instructor. I did so and, though I said nothing, Mr. Kerr really set out to give me the works. He yelled and cursed me every day for the next three weeks and taught me nothing. He'd usually have me fly to an auxiliary field, where he'd get out and sleep under a tree while I flew around the countryside until near the end of our two-hour flying period, when I'd pick him up and return to home base. My classmate was assigned to another instructor and passed the course. Our primary training airplane was the Boeing-built PT-17 Stearman, and it was perfect for training. You could do any aerial maneuver and make almost any mistake, and it would forgive you and get you safely back on the ground.

During the fall of 1941, our base operated only five days a week and our tactical officers all went home on Friday afternoons. We cadets soon learned that we could slip out through the back fence in civvies and go to town for Saturday night. My best girlfriend, Constance Bailey, was attending graduate school at the University of Arkansas, and they were scheduled to play Texas A&M in Little Rock on December 6, 1941. We agreed to meet in Little Rock on Friday evening along with our old college friend Joe Crane, who was attending flying school in Sikeston, Missouri, and would be en route to Randolph Field, Texas, that weekend. Connie was to bring a friend along for Joe.

I slipped out early that Friday and hitchhiked to Little Rock.

In addition to the Arkansas-Texas A&M game, the state fair was on, with a big rodeo scheduled for Friday and Saturday nights. I never encountered as many drunks or as much horse manure on the streets in my life. Connie, Joe, his date, and I had a wonderful weekend. We said our goodbyes on Sunday morning, December 7, 1941, my twenty-third birthday, and departed. I hitchhiked back to Canton and arrived at my barracks about 5 P.M. I had undressed and headed to the showers when Clyde Collins, my bunkmate, said he'd heard on the radio that the Japs had attacked Pearl Harbor and that all military personnel were ordered to report to their respective posts. I didn't even know where Pearl Harbor was or what it was. I'd been AWOL all weekend and had no idea what would ensue.

About 6 P.M. our officers arrived and shortly ordered us into formation. They told us that the United States was under attack and that we would have to establish a guard around the base. They issued us all rifles with live ammo and gave us a fifteen-minute instruction on how to load and unload them. That night one of the cadets was assigned to guard the fuel farm, which consisted of four large, aboveground fuel tanks, the surrounding surface of which was covered with gravel. He was told that if he heard anyone enter the area, he should order them to halt and should call the guard. If they did not halt, he was to shoot them. Late that night, a dog entered the area and, when it failed to halt as ordered, the cadet began to fire in the direction of what he thought were footsteps—in and among the fuel tanks. Why they didn't catch fire I'll never know, for the bullets were caroming off the round metal tanks in all directions! (He somehow missed the dog.) From that night on, we did guard duty with unloaded rifles.

The attack on Pearl Harbor brought many changes to our operations. We were ordered to dispose of our automobiles and to ship all of our civilian clothes home. Flight training was now conducted seven days a week, and our tactical officers were placed on a seven-day work week.

We finished the course in early January 1942 and headed off

for the U.S. Army Air Corps Flying Training School at the still unfinished airfield at Greenville, Mississippi, on the banks of the Mississippi River. We were in the heart of the Mississippi Delta country in the middle of a very wet winter. The base roads and walks were yet to be paved, and the Mississippi mud stuck to our shoes like gumbo. The mess halls weren't ready yet either, and I recall one breakfast when we ate dry cereal with water because someone had failed to procure milk.

Here we trained in the BT-13, a Chance Vought all-metal airplane with a Wright 450-horsepower engine, otherwise known as the "Maytag Messerschmitt." It was a great airplane to fly and again very forgiving. My instructor was Frank Bailey. He was also my squadron commander and the son of the governor of Arkansas. I was his only student, and he was a wonderful instructor. My only problem was that his many other duties prevented him from flying with me as much as he should have, and I found myself out flying around on my own, buzzing steamboats on the river instead of practicing required maneuvers.

Soon the Pearl Harbor attack scare subsided, and we returned to a five-day week to give the maintenance section the weekend to get our airplanes ready. We were then permitted to go into town on Saturdays. The folks in Greenville were wonderful to us, inviting us into their homes and treating us like royalty. Ken Reecher, a classmate from Hagerstown, Maryland, had hidden his Chevy coupe in a garage in town and, though we'd been told not to leave Greenville, four of us decided one Saturday night to go to Memphis, about ninety miles away. We drove to the Peabody Hotel and proceeded to the nightclub on the roof widely known as "The Top of the Peabody." The orchestra was playing, and the action looked inviting. As we stood near the entrance in our cadet uniforms, a gentleman approached us and said, "Boys, do you have a table in there?" We replied, "No sir." He said, "You see that table in front near the band, it's yours. Do you have any girls?" "No sir," we replied. He said, "Here, take my date," and pushed his girl to us. Then he said, "I see you haven't any whiskey," so he handed me a fifth of Three Feathers Blended Bourbon Whiskey.

We had a ball, to say the least. The lights were turned down and the spinning crystal ball reflected spots of light moving around the walls. I was dancing with "our date" when suddenly someone tapped me on the shoulder. I turned and there stood Lieutenant Fellows, an instructor at our base. He said, "Cadet McLaughlin, what in the hell are you doing here?" My heart sank, for this was a perfect washout case. I weakly replied with some embarrassment, trying to apologize for the error of our ways. He laughed and danced on by and was decent enough not to report us. Though we had a great evening, we didn't try that again.

We graduated in late February and reported to a new and yet unfinished base in Columbus, Mississippi. There we began training in twin-engine airplanes, first in the AT-17 Cessna, a cloth-covered airplane, underpowered but easy to handle. Later in the course they brought in a few new Lockheed Hudson airplanes that were built for the British. They were very awkward to handle on the ground, because you had to pull back on a handbrake then depress the rudder pedals to steer the plane. In the air, however, they were great and more powerful than any aircraft I'd flown.

In the final phase or our flight training we were required to fly a three-hour navigational cross-country flight to prove our prowess in finding our way through the skies. We were teamed up, with two pilots per plane. My partner for the flight was Charles Kelly from Plain Dealing, Louisiana, a good friend and later a squadron mate in the 92nd Bomb Group in England. None of us had received any instruction on instrument flying.

After briefing, we took off in slightly reduced visibility of about seven miles on the first leg of our flight. We landed after reaching the second airfield en route, and after refueling, we took off on the final leg back to Columbus Army Airfield. Soon we began to notice greatly reduced visibility. We were flying in fog with about one and a half miles of visibility and sometimes much less. Unable to see the various features of the terrain, we became totally lost. Suddenly, under our right wing, I saw a small town with a large water tank in midtown. Kelly was at the controls, and I alerted him and suggested he circle the water tank because I thought I could see the name of the town on the water tank. He turned and put the airplane into a dive toward the tank. As we came closer to the tank, there, clearly, were large letters that read: "Hudson Bay Flour." Not a clue in sight as to the name of the town.

We continued our flight on a time, airspeed, and distance, and as our estimated time of arrival neared we flew into considerably better weather and better visibility and arrived back at home on time.

Upon arrival we found our instructors wringing their hands and very worried. No one had anticipated bad weather, and they'd dispatched fifty airplanes all over northern Mississippi and Alabama. About half had gotten lost and landed in any field they could find, and the other half had not been heard from. Fear was evident on all the lieutenants' faces, for not only might a number of cadets be lost but also the airplanes. Thoughts of courts-martial haunted the backroads of their minds. Luckily, everyone got back without mishap. There were no more cross-country flights.

Ours was the first class to train at Columbus, and like Greenville, it was not finished upon our arrival. The place was a sea of mud. Capt. William Q. Rankin was the commandant. He was a tall, impressive officer with great military bearing who ran a tight ship. He appeared to be a very senior captain, probably an ROTC officer of an early thirties college class. He had a very ruddy complexion, and his eyes always looked like slits, as if slightly swollen and as if he might have consumed a fifth of whiskey the night before. He was all business, and we cadets promptly named him "BB Eyes" for the comic strip character in Dick Tracy. All of the base lieutenants were afraid of him and avoided him whenever possible.

As graduation week approached, I came into my barracks one afternoon and several of my colleagues were gathered around the bulletin board and promptly notified me that there was a notice for me to report to the commandant's office at 1600 hours. They began kidding me about washing out.

I immediately showered, put on my class A uniform, made certain my shoes were shined, and headed for the commandant's office, as bewildered as I'd ever been in my life. I reviewed all of my recent activities, including invitations to Saturday night dances at Mississippi State College for Women, at which one or two cadets had gotten into trouble for breaking the rules, but nothing seemed to call for a meeting with Captain Rankin.

I walked into the Commandant's office and saluted the second lieutanant adjutant in the outer office. He immediately began to lecture me on what my conduct should be while meeting with Captain Rankin. He stressed every aspect of military courtesy and cautioned me to be most careful of what I said. I asked him what the meeting was about, but he had no idea.

A few minutes later Captain Rankin arrived and gave the lieutenant a verbal lashing the likes of which I'd never heard before. He then put him in a brace and turned to me and said, "Take the seat in front of my desk, Cadet McLaughlin." I answered, "Yes sir," and sat down across the desk from the commander, with the lieutenant standing stiffly in a brace behind me.

Captain Rankin then turned to me and said, "You know, Cadet McLaughlin, we're preparing for the graduation ceremonies of your class next week and the commanding general of the Fifth U.S. Army Air Corps Service Command will be here to address your class. We need to select a cadet to represent the class and speak in response to the general's address. We have examined your records and note that you are a member of Phi Beta Kappa and have chosen you as the outstanding member of your class. You should prepare a response of not more than ten minutes and be prepared to speak next Saturday at the graduation."

To say the least I was befuddled, but I'd already made up my mind that I was going to say "Yes sir" to anything he said, so without hesitation I answered, "Yes sir."

On my way back to my barracks, I couldn't believe what I'd heard. I was certain I'd spelled it out very plainly "Fi Batar Kappar" on my personal history forms back at Fort Hayes. How could anyone mistake that for the academic honorary? Bobbie Corrie and Jim Congleton were West Virginians in my cadet class, and both knew what Fi Batar Kappar really was. When they told my other classmates, they all roared laughing and began giving me outlandish ideas for my speech. Luckily, program changes were made at the last minute, and the first class to graduate from Columbus Army Air Field Mississippi did so on April 29, 1942, without the advantage of my remarks.

We had finished our training requirements two weeks earlier, as had all the other advanced flying school cadets in the Southeast Training Command. They were all given two weeks leave before reporting to their new assignments. But Lt. Col. Joe Duckworth, a chief pilot for Eastern Airlines, had been sent to our base to establish an instrument flying training course. He had been unable to get his school open in time to reach our class, so it was decided to cancel our leaves. Cadet morale hit the bottom; everyone was disappointed. We'd been in school without letup for eight months, and we were all looking forward to going home.

We grudgingly took an eight-hour-per-day crash course on instrument flying. While most of us bitched and complained, we began to realize the man was trying to save our lives. He was an excellent teacher, knew his subject thoroughly, and also had years of actual experience to draw from. In the years that followed, I would remember and appreciate what he was trying to give us. He later established the U.S. Army Air Corps Instrument School at Tyler, Texas, which set the standards for all such schools throughout the U.S. military.

April 29, 1942, became a milestone in my aviation and military career, for on that day I received orders commissioning me as a second lieutenant in the U.S. Army, another order placing me on flying status, and a third ordering me to proceed to MacDill Army Air Field, Tampa, Florida, where I was to report to the commanding officer of the 92nd Bomb Group (Heavy). I was twenty-three years of age and had a steady job making $250 per month plus $90 per month flight pay. For a youngster who had grown up through the Great Depression, I felt I had the world by the tail. After graduation on the morning of April 29, I bid my parents goodbye and joined my friend Kenneth Reecher for the trip to MacDill.

3

Off We Go

On the morning of April 30, I found the headquarters of the 92nd Bomb Group on the second floor of Hanger No. 2, MacDill Army Air Field, and reported to the commanding officer, Col. James S. Sutton. He greeted me cordially and assigned me to the 407th Bomb Squad (Heavy) and introduced me to its commander, Capt. William M. Reid. Captain Reid was also very cordial and, as I was the newest second lieutenant aboard, he assigned me as airdrome officer for the following day. When I reported for duty, I learned that Captain Reid had been demoted to the rank of first lieutenant. I was astounded, until two days later, when he was assigned back to captain. He had gained Regular Army status through what in those days was known as the Thomasan Act and had to go back to his regular commission rank of first lieutenant. He would become a lieutenant colonel before we left the States for England three months later.

Within the week I was placed on the Link Instrument Training Schedule, and as a new second lieutenant my scheduled link training periods were 1 and 2 in the morning. I was also assigned as a B-17 copilot. I was on top of the world. I enjoyed Tampa nightlife, until it was time to report for link training. Our first pilots were from the late 1941 and the early 1942 flying classes and had barely been checked out in the B-17. So we all learned to fly the B-17 together. Our squadron had four B-17Es, and they had been heavily flown in pilot checkout duty, which meant they'd taken a helluva beating with hard landings, had been run off the runways, and had their brakes regularly burned out. Most of our flying was around the airfield traffic pattern, and I do recall one flight to about twenty thousand feet and one bombing flight where we bombed, at low level, a paint slick on Tampa Bay.

After three weeks, we moved to the airport at Sarasota, Florida, for field training. We were assigned to tents, but the war scare had sent all of the Florida snowbirds home early and furnished apartments were plentiful. Lt. Jim Foster of New Castle, Pennsylvania, and I rented a lovely six-room furnished apartment for $15 per week.

Training at Sarasota continued, but was often interrupted by our being called out for antisubmarine patrol duty. The German subs were sinking ships all over the Gulf and Atlantic shorelines and were even broadcasting on local radio frequencies at night for short periods. One morning I was dispatched to fly to the Miami Airport to pick up airplane parts, and we were shocked to find that four different ships had been torpedoed during the night by German submarines. They had all beached themselves. All were on fire, and their passengers were being helped ashore. We knew then that we really were at war and that it was serious business.

Chasing submarines was boring and hopeless. We had no radar, and we would go on eight-hour sorties in an assigned area of the Gulf, never seeing anything. On our way back to the base just after daylight one morning someone yelled, "Submarine at 2 o'clock!" We all came awake, and sure enough, there was a sub just surfacing. As we circled to set up a bomb run on it, our navigator called, saying we were close to the U.S. Navy sub base at Key West and it might be ours. Sure enough, it was ours, and we had almost sunk it.

About June 15, we were ordered to Westover Air Base, Springfield, Massachusetts. I had made two flights as copilot for Lt. Eugene Wiley of Denver, Colorado, transferring equipment and personnel. They were long and boring, and each time, as we neared New York City, Lieutenant Wiley would drop down and we'd buzz the Empire State Building. The folks in the offices would wave as we circled them. On my final flight from Sarasota to Springfield, I was flying the airplane and Maj. Bob Keck, my squadron commander, was riding as copilot. As we neared New York City he had pushed his seat back, was reading a newspaper, and did not realize that I was descending. About the time I reached the Empire State Building, he suddenly dropped his paper, grabbed the controls and said, "What in the hell are you doing?" That was my last buzz job on New York City.

After our arrival in Springfield, Massachusetts, we continued antisub patrol flights east of Boston, again with little hope of ever seeing a German submarine. Most of us had never seen a whale before, and one afternoon, when returning from a search about two hundred miles off Boston, our bombardier suddenly yelled, "sub ahead" and began firing his machine gun. I looked out, and the "sub" suddenly exhaled—with a big water spout, as did four or five other nearby whales.

By this time we single lieutenants had met the Mt. Holyoke College girls, but we soon received orders to move to Bangor, Maine. One of the girls told us that her folks had a summer place there and that she'd soon meet us in Bangor. She brought a few college friends and opened her summer place, which was located on a lake and had a long wooden pier extending a hundred feet out into the water. Most of our officers were from the South, where swimming in June was a very normal thing. After a very amorous evening someone suggested we go for a swim in the lake. We all found some swimming gear and headed for the pier. My date, who owned the place, led the way and dived off the end of the pier, followed closely by me. I surfaced in total shock. The water was about 45 degrees, and I could hardly get my breath. To say the least our romance cooled considerably.

While in Bangor we began to ferry our beat-up B-17Es to the air depot in Middletown, Pennsylvania, and pick up the new B-17Fs, with .50-caliber machine guns in the nose compartment in place of the .30-caliber guns in the B-17Es. We were very proud of them, but it was a slow process and took nearly a month to outfit the entire group.

One of the flight leaders in my squadron was Capt. William M. Knowles. He was a very senior captain, whom we affectionately called "Pappy." He had been a swimmer in the 1936 Berlin Olympics and later a performer in Billy Rose's Aquacade at the 1939 World's Fair. For security purposes we were restricted to the base, but Captain Knowles had enough seniority to get an airplane to go to New York City on the weekends. He invited me to go with him as copilot, and I gladly accepted. We flew to Mitchell Field, Long Island, on Friday afternoon and caught the train into the city. I'd only been to New York once before and knew nothing about the place. We caught a cab directly to Radio City Music Hall.

I followed him through the stage door and up a couple of flights of stairs, then directly toward the ongoing performance. He approached a pretty lady who was attentively watching the show, threw his arms around her and gave her a big buss and embrace. It was the beginning of a great evening. His lady friend was in charge of the Rockettes, and as they planned the evening she said to me, "Lieutenant, if you want a date just pick out one of the girls in the line." Then she suggested we go next door to a drug store and wait until the show was over. We did, and shortly the entire troop arrived. I picked out my date and was introduced to Bambi James, about as nice a girl as I ever met.

Pappy and his lady really knew Manhattan, as well as most every entertainer, band leader, and maitre d' in the city. We of course were in uniform, and New York, being one of the most hospitable cities in America, entertained us royally. We stopped in a couple of nightclubs for drinks, then went to the Astor Roof in the elegant Astor Hotel for dinner. The Harry James band was playing and we had a wonderful evening. Everything was on the house; we simply could not pay for anything. Finally, when we took the girls home, the cab fare was 40 cents. Until that point we hadn't spent a dime. Pappy said, "Cabby, you know we are on are way overseas to fight the Germans. Can't you give us a free-bie tonight?" The cabby replied, "I don't give a damn if you're going to hell. I want my 40 cents." We paid. The whole evening had cost us 40 cents! Two weeks later I accompanied him on the same trip. Another wonderful weekend with a super nice officer.

Sadly, Pappy Knowles was the first officer in my squadron to be killed after we arrived in England. The story of making wonderful acquaintances, getting to know truly special fellows, only to have them killed suddenly in the skies, would repeat itself all too often in the months to come.

As soon as my squadron got its new airplanes, our operations officer, Capt. James Griffith, formerly of Princeton, West Virginia, scheduled us for long over-water cruise-control flights to make sure we knew how to conserve fuel in flight and to be certain that we could fly two thousand miles nonstop. I flew with Lt. Tom Hulings, from Bangor, Maine, to Bermuda and back to Washington, D.C. By the time we arrived in Washington and got to the Occidental Restaurant for dinner we'd been up about twenty hours. I fell asleep in the chair while waiting to be served dinner.

On August 12, the 326th Squadron of our group departed for Gander Airbase, Newfoundland, and on to England. My squadron, the 407th, departed last, on August 25, landing in Gander that afternoon. Weather problems kept us there that night, and we prepared for a 10 P.M. takeoff the following day.

The main runway at Gander was five thousand feet long and five hundred feet wide, to accommodate airplanes trying to land in the frequent heavy fogs of that area. The runway had about a one-foot depression near its center, and its east end extended almost to the ocean, with a four-foot fence at the end and many large boulders along the shore just beyond the end of the runway.

A heavy summer shower came up about thirty minutes before our takeoff and filled every low area on the field at Gander with fresh rainwater. We taxied out to the west end of the runway, being the first of our squadron for takeoff. Our squadron maintenance chief had overloaded our ship with extra airplane parts, tools, and sheets of half-inch steel plate standing on edge in the bomb-bay catwalk. Then the British Operations people in Gander asked us to take on some sacks of mail and sacks of coffee and tea. Knowing nothing about weight and balance procedures in those days, we let them throw it all in. With an extra five hundred gallons of fuel in our bomb bay tanks, we were hopelessly overloaded. As Major Keck advanced the throttles, we began to rumble down the runway. About the time the airplane began to act as if it might fly, we hit the water that had gathered in the center of the runway. In the next two hundred feet we dropped from 65 to 45 miles per hour airspeed.

Why we didn't stop and taxi back and take off down the bare side of the runway I'll never know, but as we emerged from the small lake in the runway we had about twenty-five hundred feet of runway left, and Major Keck held the throttles against the forward stops. With about five hundred feet of runway left he pulled her off the ground and we staggered about three feet over the fence and the huge boulders beyond. After a short climb out, we began a left turn to circle and pick up our wingmen. I knew then that the B-17 had to be the most forgiving airplane ever built for in any other airplane we'd have died at the end of that runway. As we departed, I looked back at the shore and wondered if I'd ever see America again.

We flew, as we had been briefed, in a loose formation at nine thousand feet above sea level. We turned our directional radio compasses to a strong low-frequency British radio station known as Stornaway, located north of Scotland, from which we could receive directional signals and confirm our positions en route. The only minor problems encountered were rain showers and the Northern Lights, an unusual and beautiful sight.

About halfway across the North Atlantic, I climbed out of the seat to stretch my legs. I went below to the navigator's position and found our navigator, Lt. Hubert Miller, up in the dome taking an astro (astronomical navigation) shot. Lieutenant Miller was about six feet, four inches tall and weighed about 250 pounds. He'd played tackle for Clemson University, as I recall, and had been out of navigation school only ninety days, and I'm certain this was his first opportunity to shoot a night astro shot since school. His aerial maps were spread across the navigator's table, which was only a total of about sixteen by twenty-six inches. When he climbed out of the astro dome, I said, "Miller, where are we?" He placed his right hand, which covered the whole north Atlantic, on the middle of the ocean on his map and said very authoritatively, "Right there. Right there." I laughed and checked his radio compass indicator, which was also slaved to the main radio receiver. It had settled down considerably once we'd passed the rain showers and was steadily showing Stornoway at about ten degrees to our left.

Soon the sky ahead began to brighten as the morning dawned, and shortly the green fields of County Galway were passing beneath us. (I would see them again under less charming circumstances.) An hour later we were on the ground at Prestwick, Scotland, with all of our airplanes intact. It was a tired but joyful group, to say the least.

The following day, Sunday, August 27, 1942, we flew to our home base, Bovingdon, Hertfordshire, England, about twenty miles northwest of London. As we were traveling to our newly assigned barracks we crossed the Village Green, and there we saw the British Home Guard practicing defensive maneuvers against a German invasion. I was shocked, for those guardsmen were all my father's age or older. Many had gray hair protruding from beneath their camouflaged helmets. All of the road signs had been removed, and I began to really feel for these poor British people and for once felt better about being there to try to help them.

A few minutes after arriving in my room, my squadron mate and flying classmate Jimmy Dempsey, from Wilson, North Carolina, came in, took me aside, and whispered to me, saying, "Let's go to London tonight. We've no assignments yet, and things are so screwed up they'll never miss us." It sounded good to me, so out the back we went to the Hemel Hempstead rail station and on to London town.

Until that time there had been almost no Americans in London. Londoners were very hospitable and anxious to meet their new allies and especially to borrow our cigarettes, which were a real luxury compared to theirs. We visited two or three pubs, I joined the Old White Club, off Piccadilly Circus, and we had dinner at the Old Quebec Club, then spent the night at the Grosvernor House hotel.

The next morning we caught the train back to the base and walked into a very cool reception from our squadron commander, who was suggesting that our little sojourn amounted to absence without leave and that a summary court-martial would be appropriate. We were warned not to leave base until a decision was made on our fate. After a couple weeks of needling and teasing by our squadron mates, the matter died a natural death.

During September and October, our squadron would fly four combat missions, three diversions, lose two combat crews in combat, plus Sgt. Archie Cothren from my crew and Capt. William M. Knowles. "Pappy" Knowles took off in a P-40 fighter to make some gunnery passes at one of our group-flying training formations. In pulling out of a dive he apparently tried to roll it, hit a high-speed stall, and dove onto the railroad tracks below. We all went to the American Cemetery at Maddingly for his funeral, for everyone loved him.

In the meantime, Gen. Ira C. Eaker, commanding general of

the 8th Air Force Bomber Command, decided that a center was needed to provide orientation for new crews and new groups coming into the 8th Air Force. Flying in England was difficult in that the Royal Air Force had a set of tried and true rules by which to reach Air-Sea Rescue in order to get a radio fix or a QDM (direction when lost). Our group established the school at Bovingdon Airdrome. It was known as the 1/11th Combat Crew Replacement Center.

During that period the first entertainers arrived from the States, including Merle Oberon, Al Jolson, Mitzi Mayfair, and Kay Francis. Our most distinguished visitor was Eleanor Roosevelt, who came to visit her son, Lt. Col. Elliot Roosevelt, who was training with us.

4

Torch

In mid-October, Lt. Tom Hullings and I were called to base operations and told to take a B-17 named *Flaming Jenny* to the American air depot at Burtonwood, England, near Liverpool, await its reconfiguration, and return it to Bovingdon Airdrome. Liverpool was a boring place to be, everyone was working, there was little entertainment, and, of course, the beer was warm. About the first of November our airplane was ready, and we immediately headed back to Bovingdon. They had added a bomb bay fuel tank to give it greater range, two lounge chairs on the left side of the bomb bay fastened to a substantial wooden floor, and a table that folded down from the wall between the two chairs. Each chair had a window. It had to be the only B-17 in the world with windows in the bomb bay. It also had another lounge chair opposite the radio operator's position and two more lounge chairs in the waist gunner's area. I wondered if it was being readied to take some big shots to America and how I might go about getting assigned to that flight.

After we landed in Bovingdon, Capt. Dave Alford, the base operations officer, told us to prepare to deliver the airplane to the airdrome at Port Wreath, in extreme southwest England, near

Land's End. The next morning I packed enough clothes for a stay of a night or two, and we flew to Port Wreath. There we reported to a very senior Air Corps colonel with the expectation of turning the airplane over to whomever he designated to receive it and then to find our way back to Bovingdon. The Colonel let us know immediately that he had no one to fly the airplane, that we were on extended detached service and could expect to fly a group of officers to Gibraltar very soon. We knew little of Gibraltar, and we began trying to find some maps and information on the airfield there.

Early the following morning, we briefed our crew on our flight to Gibraltar, picked up some sandwiches and coffee, checked our airplane, and awaited the arrival of our passengers, who turned out to be Gen. C.S. Sugden and Lt. Col. N. Barry, of the British Army, and Adm. H.M. Gale Royal and Cmdr. Browning, of the Royal Navy.

Our airplane crew consisted of Capt. Tom Hulings, pilot; 2nd Lt. J. Kemp McLaughlin (myself), copilot; 2nd Lt. Clyde Collins, navigator; S/Sgt. Edward E. Teaford, radio operator; T/Sgt. Edward D. Parrish, aerial engineer; T/Sgt. John W. Tippen, gunner; Sgt. Maurice L. Harris, gunner; Sgt. Loren E. Blanchard Jr., tail gunner; and Sgt. Johnnie J. Tucher, ball turret gunner.

The weather at the time of takeoff was restricted visibility, indefinite ceiling, and heavy fog. There were four airplanes scheduled for takeoff that morning, as I recall. Soon after the sun began to break through and the fog began to lift, the first airplane took off. Then, as we called the tower for taxi clearance, we were told to hold short of the takeoff runway, as the first airplane had crashed off the end of the runway. Shortly, the control tower cleared us for takeoff and, as we began our climb out, we could see black smoke billowing up through the fog. It was a sobering sight as we began our flight to Gibraltar, with its thirty-five hundred–foot runway with the ocean at both ends. That was a very short runway for a loaded B-17, and at an airfield that none of us had ever seen to boot.

The flight south across the Bay of Biscay was uneventful. The weather was sunny, and though we were on guard throughout, the Luftwaffe failed to come out to greet us. Later they intercepted and shot up some others making the same flight. Admiral Hale had obviously sailed through these waters many times, for he recognized every small isle and shore feature, calling each by name and assuring us that we were right on course.

We arrived over "the Rock" about 4 P.M. and circled the area twice to get a good look at the runway, which was located on the north side behind the Rock of Gibraltar. The aerodrome's airspace was too narrow to circle, because we were ordered not to fly over Spain, the border of which was close to the north side of the runway.

The sight we saw was unbelievable. The bay was jammed full of all kinds of ships, and the small airfield was covered with row after row of airplanes of every kind and description. The wind indicated a landing toward the west on the one and only runway, which began forty feet above the water on a rock cliff on the east and ran downhill into the bay on the west end. Parked airplanes lined both sides of the runway for the entire length, about fifty feet off each side. We kept our ship slow on the final approach and touched down with full flaps about four hundred feet down the runway, then we both rode the brakes to a stop a few hundred feet from the west end. A lead-in Jeep led us to a parking spot, and we shut her down with a sigh of relief.

Never before or since or ever again will I see the likes of Gibraltar just prior to the invasion of North Africa. That tiny British outpost was jammed with thousands of soldiers, sailors, and airmen from all over the world. The bay on the west side of the Rock held so many ships and landing craft that it looked as if one could walk across it. It was a perfect target for a bomb attack if I ever saw one, all in plain view of the Spanish, who could view it all from their side of the line that separated Gibraltar from Spain, probably less than a mile from the only runway. Why the Germans didn't send a few bombers in at night, I'll never know.

The small downtown commercial area of Gibraltar consisted of a few shops, four or five restaurants, and four or five nightclubs that sold whiskey and beer and had live music. The nightclubs had a few "B Girls" adorning their lounges, and with the thousands of military personnel in the streets, one would have expected chaos. But the British were too smart for that. They made all nightspots close at 10 P.M., and the girls had to be back across the border by 10 P.M. or lose their visas. The streets were thronged with thousands of men who'd had four or five drinks and most of whom were looking for a fight. To say the least, it was wild.

The first afternoon we were there, we noticed a group watching a P-38 flying over the field. Some said it was Col. Jimmy Doolittle, the famous leader of the carrier-launched B-25 raid on Tokyo in April 1942. He did a few acrobatics, then came in for a landing. As he taxied in near where we were standing, a command car drove up and out climbed Gen. Dwight D. Eisenhower and his retinue containing Gen. Bedell Smith and some colonels. Ike proceeded toward Doolittle's plane, and when Jimmy reached the tarmac, Ike began to give him the kind of military lecture that none of us had seen since cadet days. As Jimmy stood there in a brace, Ike proceeded to let him know that he was there to do planning and administrative duties, not fly airplanes. It was done in front of all of us lieutenants, sergeants, and privates and was most embarrassing to Doolittle as well as all of us, for Jimmy Doolittle was a genuine American hero, and every airman held him in high regard. I was turned off on Ike from that day on, after that incident, and from what I observed while working in his Allied Force Headquarters, I couldn't bring myself to vote for him ten years hence.

Col. Jimmy Doolittle was later promoted to brigadier general and appointed commanding general of the 12th Tactical Air Force for the Invasion of North Africa (Operation Torch). He was so successful that he later became commanding general of "the Mighty 8th" Air Force in England for the invasion of Europe, Operation Overlord, in 1944.

That same day we learned that we were there to fly Gen. Carl A. "Tooey" Spaatz, who was the commanding general of all U.S. Air Forces in Europe. With one day's change of clothes and no place to acquire any fresh military clothing, I wondered how I would look in my new role. We were issued field equipment, including mess gear, blankets, and the fanciest bedroll I'd ever seen. It had an air mattress and a down-filled inner liner, solid comfort.

Capt. Jack Reedy, Lt. Larry Hampton, and crew, also from our 92nd Bomb Group, had flown another reconfigured B-17 to Gibraltar, and it turned out that they would fly for General Eisenhower.

On the morning of November 8, we awakened to a strangely silent Gibraltar. All of the ships had disappeared and only a handful of airplanes remained on the airfield. They had all departed in the night or near daylight to invade Morocco and Algeria. The C-47s had carried the British, Canadian, and American paratroops to targets at Casablanca, Oran, Algiers, and other coastal areas after midnight, and the landing craft had carried infantry, engineers, and other personnel to shore landings in those areas.

We were briefed to take off on the following day for Maison Blanche, the municipal airport at Algiers. We arrived in midafternoon to find the airport under Allied control but again jammed with fighter, bomber, and transport airplanes. The field was very muddy, and when we attempted to taxi to our designated parking area we promptly became mired to the wheel hubs. Someone found a farm tractor and towed us to our parking spot, where we were again stuck deep in the mud.

That first evening and night in Algeria was a rather inhospitable one for me. We were directed to an old French barracks in which to spend the night. En route to the barracks, I passed a GI tending a fire under a fifty-five gallon drum. Everyone was emptying his rations into this drum. The sergeant told me to do the same and that we'd have hot food for dinner. I did as told and, after settling into the barracks, I returned with my mess kit to get my evening meal. The mixed rations were boiling hot and smelled great. The November evening had cooled considerably, and I looked forward to my hot meal—until I tasted it. I almost gagged. The drum had originally contained oil, and they had not thoroughly cleansed it. The food was awful. I ate a few bites and tossed it. Later, I climbed into my new bedroll on an empty stomach.

My barracks were filled with all manner of personnel: officers, sergeants, and plain old GIs, all sleeping on a concrete floor. All were bone weary and seemed to sleep right through all the coming and going and outside noises that went on all night. The next morning I arose to my usual morning ablutions. The French latrines consisted of holes in the floor that one could use Indian style. When I returned to my bunk I was stunned to learn that some needy GI had lifted my beautiful new bedroll and was long gone. I hope he enjoyed it, for as it turned out I would not need it again anyway.

For breakfast that morning I skipped the hot meal deal and enjoyed my rations cold, for I was famished. After my early breakfast, I walked around the airfield to examine the damage left from our invasion. Most buildings had bullet holes throughout, and beside one hangar stood a German Heinkel bomber, also full of bullet holes, but which was said to have just arrived from Argentina, as a Buenos Aires day-old newspaper had been found on board. It apparently had maintenance problems and had become a victim of our invasion.

Our crew met at our airplane that morning, and we were soon notified to get our possessions together—we would be billeted in town. We joined some others on a "6 by 6" Army truck and headed for Algiers, about fifteen miles away. We reported to a temporary headquarters in the Hotel Alletti and were told that our officers would be billeted in the Hotel Victoria and our enlisted crewmen in another hotel nearby. No one knew where the Victoria was located, but as we stood outside the Alletti's entrance with our baggage several youngsters showed up, begging to carry our baggage. One who could speak a few words of English, and whom we promptly labeled "Broadway Bill," said he'd take us to the Victoria. We all started down the street following Broadway Bill and, after two hours wandering around Algiers, he finally confessed he had no idea where it might be. That became lesson number one in not believing anything that anyone in Algiers told us. We finally found a local policeman who located our hotel for us.

The city of Algiers and most of the natives there were living under terrible conditions. All of North Africa had been occupied and ruled by the German army since 1940, and they had pretty well stripped the country of any materials worth having. They took all the food they could find during their retreat, and many Algerians were hungry when we arrived. Our army distributed rations to many of them for several weeks.

The Hotel Victoria turned out to be a solid, third-rate hostelry. It was a family operation of four or five stories. The furniture was ancient, the rugs bare, and the draperies moth-eaten. My room faced north toward the Mediterranean, and a pair of French doors opened onto a patio that was level with the roof of the building across the street, as all of Algiers is located on a hill facing the harbor. On top of that building sat the city's only air-raid siren, a large one with four horns, one of which pointed directly toward my room. It was so loud that I had to leave my room when it sounded, for it fairly vibrated the fillings in my teeth. German and Italian bombers paid us nuisance visits every night, setting the alarm off regularly.

Soon after settling in Algiers I became acquainted with Lt. D.V. Duff, Royal New Zealand NVR, and Lt. K.S. Upton of the Royal Australian Navy, two of the greatest gentlemen I met in the whole war. Both had been on duty with the Royal Navy for four years or more and were totally streetwise. They were five or six years older than I and took me under their wings, so to speak, and taught me the ropes. Each evening I would meet them at the Hotel Alletti, and we'd work our way through our favorite bars to the hotel of the British Navy headquarters, which always had excellent food. One of our favorite stops was a bar that a local sheik frequented with his retinue of eunuchs. They sat in a circle on pillows with a large water pipe in the center, drinking and smoking and living it up. These bars had no whiskey or bourbon, but the best champagne and wines were a half cent per glass, and even we second lieutenants could afford that.

One such evening, as we walked along the waterfront, we noticed the harbor was littered with paper. A large freighter was being unloaded, and we learned that it had been hit in the forward hold where all the mail was stored, and what we were seeing was our mail from home floating on the bay. As we lamented this loss, the pier crane suddenly lifted high an olive-drab Cadillac from the center hold. It was Ike's staff car. With a few well-chosen expletives, Duff began to needle me over the fact that the Axis had destroyed our mail instead of Ike's Cadillac. When I began to complain because I had not heard from home in two months, Duff retorted, "Poor old Mac hasn't heard from home in two months. When did you last hear from home, Upton? Six months ago?" Duff and Upton had left the Pacific in June, and their mail had not yet caught up with them.

We became fast friends, and one evening after several drinks we were having dinner in the British naval officers' mess with a couple of English naval lieutenants whom my Australian friends had dubbed "blue bloods." During the evening one of the English naval officers referred to me as "just another bloody provincial." With that, Duff rose and slugged his English colleague, knocking him out of his chair and onto the floor, exclaiming that "Moc," as he called me, was not a bloody provincial, that I was "a bloody American." I was totally embarrassed and thought nothing of the reference, but Duff took it as an insult to me and was not about to sit there and let this lieutenant get away with it. I also suspect that most New Zealanders, Aussies, South Africans, Canadians, etc. enjoyed any excuse to jump a "blue blood. "

Another evening we were down near the waterfront, en route to our favorite bar, and noted hundreds of GIs in full battle dress, waiting near a rail head. Soon a long train came backing in and, when it came to a stop, several soldiers were recruited to help unload hundreds of wounded American soldiers sent back from the Tunisian battle front. This scene put terror in the hearts of the young soldiers waiting to entrain. At the same time, thousands of Italian prisoners were disembarking, singing and laughing and delighted to be out of war. I heard one shout to our troops, "So long, Yanks, we're going to Broadway."

Our assignment to fly for General Spaatz turned out to be a great experience. His headquarters was located with the Allied Force Headquarters in the St. George Hotel at the very top of the hill overlooking the city, the harbor, and the Mediterranean. The office consisted of General Spaatz, his chief of staff, Col. Edwin "Ted" Curtis (president of Eastman Kodak and a World War I flying mate of Tooey's), and a warrant officer who was in reality a male secretary. General Spaatz and Ted Curtis treated us as if we were their sons.

General Spaatz knew that we had little flying experience and no instrument training. The area we'd be flying in contained the Atlas Mountains, which were ten thousand to twelve thousand feet high, and remembering that army regulations required every pilot to fly and record four hours each month to collect flight pay, he said, as he came aboard for his first flight with us, "Gentlemen, I want you to always remember two rules when I'm flying with you. Number one, don't ever fly through a cloud when I'm aboard, and number two, don't ever fail to put my name on the Airplane Form 1." We laughed a lot about those rules, but we never failed him.

Each Wednesday we were dispatched to Casablanca, which in military terms was known as the Zone of Interior and was the port into which military supplies of all kinds were stockpiled. Gen. George S. Patton Jr. had been relegated to the Post Zone of

Interior Command and was fuming mad at being forced to cool his heels in Casablanca while the action took place in Tunisia.

General Spaatz had given me a written note to the quartermaster that read simply, "Give this Lt. anything he wants, signed Tooey Spaatz, B/G, USA." The standard order of supplies each week consisted of whatever Ike's staff had ordered, the things we needed for our crew and airplane, and eight cases of whiskey—one half scotch and one half bourbon. After each trip Colonel Curtis always gave me a quart of bourbon. I was the only second lieutenant in Algiers who had any whiskey, which greatly enhanced my status.

Since the trip from Algiers to Casablanca was quite long, we usually spent the night. On our first trip we learned that the only officers' mess was in a hotel downtown. But the officer in charge would not admit us because we were not dressed in Class A uniforms. General Patton would not permit any officer to eat in the mess unless he was in a dress uniform. When we returned and reported this incident, General Spaatz blew up, saying, "Why that old SOB! What does he think he's trying to do?"

A few days later the German Army drove our forces out of the Kasserine Pass and captured and killed a lot of Americans. Ike then ordered Patton to take charge of our combat forces in the field. As soon as he arrived, the German air force pinned his forces down and stopped him cold. On the following Monday morning, I received a call to report to General Spaatz's office immediately. I was a little alarmed and wondered if they might have learned of some of my evening activities in town with Duff and Upton.

I arrived in the office with Capt. Tom Hulings and found General Spaatz seated at his desk with Colonel Curtis standing beside him holding a piece of paper. As Captain Hulings and I stepped to the desk and saluted, Colonel Curtis handed us the paper he was holding. It was a wire from Patton to Ike, screaming for air cover, and it had been sent on to Spaatz to answer. Ted Curtis, with a big grin on his face, handed us the wire and said,

"Boys, here's a wire from that SOB who wouldn't let you in the mess at Casablanca, and we think you ought to answer it." Two years later, General Patton would send me a case of cognac in appreciation for my bomb group's support of his Army corps around Aachen, Germany.

We flew General Spaatz to visit Air Corps units all around North Africa. One day we took him to visit a P-40 group near Telergma. It was as primitive a place as could be. Not a single building on the field. The aviation engineers had simply scraped the desert floor for the runway and dug some basement-like excavations for a mess, operations, and headquarters. Each had canvas and camouflaged roofs. The officers and airmen all lived in foxholes dispersed around the field. Airplane maintenance included changing spark plugs and minor light maintenance. If an airplane had anything critically wrong, they just pushed it out into the desert and got a new machine ready.

While General Spaatz was handing out medals the air-raid alarm sounded. Four two-ship flights of P-40s took off to defend the place. We climbed aboard our B-17 and had it ready to go if necessary. Soon the "all clear" signal sounded, and the P-40s landed without incident.

While on another trip to Biskra, to visit two B-17 groups (the 301st and 97th) and two P-38 groups, we were crossing the Atlas Mountains at about 12,000 feet when suddenly a British Spitfire came alongside and waggled his wings. He then pulled out away from us and proceeded to execute a perfect eight-point roll. It was Brig. Gen. Jimmy Doolittle, en route to meet us there for an official visit.

Biskra is located in southern Algeria, just south of the Atlas Mountains on the edge of the Sahara Desert. Our bomber and fighter groups were moved there to get them away from the muddy landing fields of the sea plain. Also they were beyond the reach of enemy bombers. Upon our arrival, General Spaatz was met by the group commanders and whisked away to the troops who awaited him. As we were buttoning up our airplane, someone directed my attention to a large camel train plodding toward us from the desert.

It was a sight I've long remembered. About fifty camels, each heavily laden, began circling nearby. About every fifth camel had a small black boy aboard. On command, all of the camels lay down in a huge circle. The black boys unloaded them and fed them. It was early December, and the evening temperature was probably around fifty degrees. The camel drivers wore only loincloths. As soon as each had fed his last camel, he took his own food and crawled up between the back legs of a large female camel. A warm and cozy spot to spend the night. The old Arab in bloomers who led the caravan pitched a small tent and soon had a fire burning in front, with his personal servant cooking their dinner.

One morning we were ordered to fly Gen. Bedell Smith to Oran, Algeria. A German sub had sunk an Allied ship in that area, and we were to pick up some of the rescued passengers. We arrived in Oran about noon. It was a cold and rainy December day, and the airport was a sea of mud. We parked our airplane near the operations building and went inside. There we met our passengers, which included the first WACs to arrive in the North Africa/European Theater. They were Mattie Pinettie, a former college professor from the University of Maine, Martha Rogers, Alene Drezmal, Ruth M. Briggs, Louise Anderson, and Ike's personal chauffeur, Kay Summersby. Gen. Bedell Smith shepherded them aboard. They were putting up a pretty good front, for in reality they had been through a rough experience. Their ship had been torpedoed the night before. They lost most of their clothes and were especially bemoaning the loss of their nylon stockings, which were almost unavailable in World War II. They had then been rescued from the ship and brought to Oran, where we picked them up.

Gen. Bedell Smith got them onboard our plane and began chomping at the bit to take off. It was pouring rain and every depression on the field was full of water. Outside of the base operations building, from which we filed our flight plan, was an antiaircraft gun emplacement. Its two 20mm guns were set in a bunker that was four feet deep, full of rainwater, and now looked just like every other puddle on the field. Our navigator emerged from the building and hurriedly made a direct path to our airplane. Without realizing it, he stepped into the gun emplacement and went in up to his waist. He then, of course, had to retreat to the operations building to try to dry himself. General Smith blew up. He wanted us to take off and leave him. He fussed and fumed until Lt. Clyde Collins, still soaking wet, made it back to the airplane. I crossed Bedell Smith off my list that afternoon.

These WACs and Kay Summersby were delightful people. All were full of personality and humor, even though they had been through a very fearful experience the night before.

After we landed back at Maison Blanche, the airport at Algiers, Kay Summersby and the other WACs were taken to the Glycine Clinic, where they were permanently quartered. It was within walking distance of the Allied Force Headquarters in the St. George Hotel. They all became administrative assistants to Ike's top staff officers. Since all the roads in Algeria were either impassable or too dangerous for any automobile, I was never certain what Kay Summersby's duties were.

With various fighters and bomber groups stationed across North Africa, logistical problems arose in trying to keep them supplied, particularly with fuel. All of our fuel was shipped in five-gallon cans. Our B-17 burned nearly two hundred gallons per hour, and a five- to six-hour round trip took one thousand to two thousand gallons of fuel. It took our entire crew a couple of hours each time to refuel the airplane. Pouring five gallons of fuel, one can at a time, was an exasperating business.

The army had a transportation battalion at Maison Blanche Airport made up of black troops. The Army was racially segregated then. This battalion hauled all the fuel to these air groups. The roads were nearly all unimproved then, and with the winter rains, transporting fuel was always a problem. The French and particularly the North African Arabs had little regard for black people and often assaulted or killed them on sight. Often when these supply convoys were sent out we'd be dispatched to fly their route and see how they were getting along. Many times we'd find them with trucks that had failed for some reason lashed to the truck ahead or sometimes three or four trucks lashed together, making their way through the desert or mountains. Other times, when a truck broke down, the next truck just picked up the driver and left the truck. The natives soon got wise to this, for a truckload of gasoline could make a poor rural Arab rich. Soon they were shooting at the convoys in an attempt to steal the fuel. The black truck drivers were terrified.

During December, Gen. Mark Clark was assembling his 5th Army near Ouijda, Morocco, and during that same period he served as Ike's emissary to various tribes and rural regions of Algeria and Morocco. He was a regular passenger with us and about the most admirable senior officer I met during the war. He'd played a key role in paving the way for our invasion and was a favorite of the French in North Africa. On one such trip to visit his army in training, I was riding in the front seat of the staff car, with General Clark and the colonel in charge riding in the back seat, en route from the airfield to the camp. As we came over a rise we noticed a single one-story building with three or more GIs standing in line at the door. General Clark asked the colonel what that building was, and the colonel embarrassingly explained that there'd been several American GIs who'd caught strange venereal diseases and, thus, were permanently lost from further duty, so the medics had hired several local girls who'd passed their medical exams and established a bordello. General Clark, being the gentlemen that he was, did not press his inquiry further. He was the finest general officer I met during World War II.

Lieutenants Duff and Upton had been taking me to the British naval officers' mess each evening, where we had delicious dinners, so I attempted to return their favors by inviting them up to our officers' mess at Allied Force Headquarters for Thanksgiving. It had been announced that we'd have turkey that day. We had hiked for most of an hour up those steep streets to the St. George, and we arrived in the mess at the appointed hour, only to find that we were having spam in lieu of turkey. An announcement was made that, since there wasn't enough turkey for all the troops in the field, Ike had ordered that the headquarters would do without turkey. Duff and Upton never let me live it down. The other naval officers who heard about it couldn't believe it happened.

The first anniversary of the Pearl Harbor attack, December 7, 1942, was celebrated with prayer and reverence. Americans were dying in battles on both sides of the world. We were struggling in Tunisia, and the American plight seemed grim everywhere. It was also my twenty-fourth birthday, and I hadn't heard from home in nearly three months.

Early in January 1943 we were alerted to prepare for a trip to Casablanca. Our passengers turned out to be two colonels and Lt. Louise Anderson, the only woman to attend the historic Casablanca Conference.

5

Err'n in Erin

Upon our return from Casablanca we were again alerted for another trip, this time to England. We were to be going back to our home base. I bought a bushel of oranges and two cases of wine for my mates back at Bovingdon. Our passengers were Lt. Gen. Jacob Devers, at that time commander of American Forces in the European Theater of Operations, and his staff, consisting of Brig. Gen. Gladeon M. Barnes, Col. William T. Sexton, Maj. Gen. Edward McBrooks, and Maj. Earl Hormell, his aviation advisor.

We departed Algiers in the early afternoon for Gibraltar, arriving about 5 P.M. We refueled, ate dinner, and began working up our flight plan, which would take us west from Gibraltar, past Portugal, then north across the Bay of Biscay to the English Channel, then northeast to Bovingdon Airport, just northwest of London.

We delayed our takeoff from Gibraltar until after midnight in order to evade the German fighters and arrive in England well after daylight. Winter dawn didn't arrive until after 8 A.M. (Double Daylight Saving Time). The flight plan called for about seven and a half hours for the entire trip. We also would be flying through a cold front that was drifting southeast across England into France and would present us with head winds and navigation problems all the way. We got off about 2 A.M. on January 15 and began what seemed to be an uneventful flight. We hit the cold front in the Bay of Biscay and rocked along in it most of the night. Our navigator was unable to shoot any astro shots because of cloud cover.

Shortly after daylight, we encountered a broken-to-scattered cloud deck below our nine thousand–foot mean sea flight level, and about 9:15 A.M. our navigator gave us a northeasterly heading for a southwest England landfall thirty minutes later. After we turned to our northeasterly heading, General Devers's aide and air advisor pilot, Major Hormell, came into the cockpit and checked our new heading. He then said he was worried that our headwinds had slowed our ground speed so much that our new northeasterly heading might result in a landfall on the Nazi-held Brest Peninsula instead of southwest England, and that German coastal guns might shoot us down.

His argument was a valid one in the sense that the coast-lines and terrain were similar, making an identification error possible. Additionally, there was the danger of having the European Theater commander and his staff killed, or worse, captured. He suggested that we turn to a westerly heading for thirty minutes, then north for thirty minutes, then easterly to make sure we hit England instead of France. Lt. Clyde Collins, our navigator, objected, saying we should fly out our flight plan and check the coast features for definite identification before we entered. In the meantime, Staff Sergeant Teaford, our radio operator, had tried to get us a QDM (Radio Directional Course) from RAF radio stations, but an RAF night-bombing raid was returning, and the stations by regulation would not honor our calls. Lieutenant Hulings decided to take the major's advice. We returned to a westerly heading, a move that later proved disastrous.

We flew our westerly heading back into the Atlantic, then north, then back on an easterly heading, and made landfall shortly after 11 A.M. We had obviously hit Ireland, but our navigator had no maps of Ireland and could not positively identify anything. We were in the Galway Bay area, but none of us had ever been to Ireland and, with no maps to identify the towns, bays, and streams, we couldn't be sure. As we circled the area, we saw some peat bogs. One of our passengers was British Flying Sgt. R.C. Bolland, hitchhiking his way home from a three-year tour as a Spitfire pilot on Malta. When he saw the peat bogs, he said he thought it was Scotland, suggesting the idea that perhaps we'd flown up the Irish Sea and warning that an eastward course that might take us from Ireland to England could also take us from Scotland toward Germany.

We then made a decision to fly north into northern Ireland, where two or three American airplane modification depots were located (the northern counties of Ireland were still part of Great Britain). Captain Hulings and I had previously flown to one of them. As we flew north, the rolling farmland began to disappear, and we found ourselves flying over a minor mountain range. By this time we'd been airborne for nearly ten hours, and we began to worry about fuel. Suddenly, one of the low-fuel warning lights flashed on, indicating about twenty minutes of remaining flight time.

Not knowing for certain how far we were from an airport, Lieutenant Hulings elected to fly toward the rolling terrain of the Galway area, in southern Ireland, where we'd have a better chance of finding a field large enough to set down on. At that time he instructed me to go back and tell General Devers of our fuel shortage and of our plan to crash-land the airplane. He also told me to tell Devers that we did have enough fuel to climb the airplane to five thousand feet above sea level and allow the general and his staff to parachute to the ground rather than face the risk of a crash landing. After I explained the situation to General Devers, he said, "Son, what are you going to do?" I said "Sir, I'm going to help Captain Hulings land this airplane." He said, "All right, son, we'll do whatever you're going to do."

When I returned to the cockpit and told Hulings of the General's decision, Hulings alerted the crew to prepare for a crash landing and to so instruct all the passengers. By this time all four red low-fuel warning lights were on, and we knew the end was near.

We circled and noted that nearly every field large enough to land an airplane on had a large post in the center. The Irish had done this to make certain that no British airplane would land without wrecking or at least incurring damage. Also, all the fences dividing the fields were of stone.

We decided on a narrow field on which we could approach and land into the westerly wind. It too had rock-wall fences, and because it was narrow, it looked longer than it actually was. It contained a few cows, but they were feeding along the southern side, which left us enough room to roll down the center. We set up a long approach and dragged our B-17 in with full flaps, landing gear down. She settled in after we crossed the eastern fence. We both stood on the brakes as the airplane hydroplaned on the wet grass for the rest of the length of the field. The landing gear was knocked off as we hurdled the far wall fence, and the airplane came to rest on its belly in the next field. I pulled back my side window and looked down and saw smoke rising from the number three engine. I panicked, tossed my chute harness, and slithered out through that window, which was about eighteen inches by eighteen inches. For fifty-five years I've wondered how a man my size could have done that.

I then ran to the rear door of the airplane and began helping our passengers out. Of the seventeen people on board, none was injured. Just after we landed, I saw an Irish Home Guard soldier with a rifle running through the trees toward us, yelling in Gaelic and waving his arms. General Spaatz had given me three letters to be delivered to Gen. Ira Eaker and two others at 8th Bomber Command. Not knowing what they contained, I was alarmed that they might fall into the wrong hands. I asked General Devers what I should do with them. He said, "Eat them." I quickly and quietly consumed them without further ado.

The Irish soldier could speak only Gaelic, and none of us could converse with him, so we began to unload our personal effects. As the local folks began gathering around, my two cases of wine and basket of fruit soon disappeared. The Irish, like the English, hadn't seen any tropical fruit since the war began. Staff Sergeant Teaford blew up the IFF (Secret Identification Equipment) so it would not be captured intact. (Each IFF set had a built-in explosive charge to ensure its destruction, if necessary.) We carried no Norden bombsight aboard this flight.

By this time, a few Irish people began to gather around us, along with a very elegant Irish lady on whose farm we had landed. She carried a stone jug of Irish whiskey and several coffee mugs. The local parish priest accompanied her. She greeted us very cordially and insisted we have a cup of whiskey. General Devers suggested we all accept her gracious hospitality, so we each had about six to eight ounces of straight Irish whiskey. It was now noon and, not having eaten since the night before, that cup of whiskey quickly wiped away my strongest apprehensions. In fact, I couldn't hit the ground with my hat and, totally relaxed, everything suddenly became kind of funny. The priest presented me with a religious medal for good luck.

Shortly the locals found some automobiles and drove us to a hotel near the town of Athenry. They immediately opened the bar, and we began to have more drinks while they prepared our lunch. By the time lunch was served we were all three sheets to the wind, and after having been up all night I could hardly keep my head up as we supped on a delicious breakfast of steak and eggs.

Shortly after we arrived at the inn, one of General Devers's staff called the American consul in Dublin and arranged for our transportation out of southern Ireland (the Irish Republic). We remained around the dining hall until after dark. Officially, southern Ireland was a neutral country, and, according to the Geneva

Convention, we were supposed to have been interned there for the rest of the war.

Early in the evening two sedans and a small bus arrived. We quickly boarded and headed for northern Ireland, arriving well after midnight. We spent the rest of that night at Langford Lodge. The following day we flew back to our home base at Bovingdon, Hertfordshire, our original destination.

After arriving back at Bovingdon, I fully expected an investigation and a formal hearing on our snafu. Except for a letter of explanation that Lt. Tom Hulings wrote, nothing happened. I'm certain that General Eaker and General Spaatz realized that our crew had only a few months' flying experience, that this flight was only the third flight over water for our navigator, and that an investigation would be a waste of time.

I was assigned to base operations as a duty pilot and spent the next three months instructing Americans transferring into the U.S. Army Air Corps from the RAF and from the Royal Canadian Air Force, along with several older colonels who were coming to the European Theater of Operations, how to fly the B-17. The transferees from the RAF and the RCAF were largely youngsters who for different reasons had been unable to join the U.S. Army Air Corps. Most had little flying experience and had not attended college. The majority were given flight-officer status, and we did our best to make B-17 copilots of them. Consequently, when several senior colonels were sent to England in early 1943 to begin the buildup of what would become the mighty 8th Air Force, most of them had never flown a B-17, so General Eaker sent them to us.

A second lieutenant with less than a year's experience teaching a group of colonels with twenty-plus years' experience presents some peculiar problems. Though most were very easy to work with, a few weren't. One colonel had flown an early B-17 at Wright Field, Ohio, in 1938. It had no turrets, guns, or ammo on board and thus was ten thousand to twenty thousand pounds lighter than the B-17Es that we had at Bovingdon. Our flight procedure around the landing pattern called for 110 miles per hour on the downwind leg, dropping to 100 on the crosswind and on to 80 to 90 miles per hour on the final approach depending on how heavily the airplane was laden. This particular colonel insisted on flying the downwind leg at 90 miles per hour, dropping to 80 or 85 on the crosswind, and on to 70 or 75 on the final approach. On the first two attempts we lost so much altitude in the turns that we could not land and had to go around for a new approach on each attempt. I was standing between the pilots' seats with this pilot in the 1st pilot's seat and an inexperienced colonel in the copilot's seat. It was a hair-raising experience. We finally succeeded on the third landing attempt by carrying 50 percent power on all four engines all the way down the final approach just before touchdown. I never heard from this fellow again, but I'd guess the odds were he ended up in a POW camp.

During this period our crew was assigned to the 1/11th Combat Crew Replacement Center, which our original 92nd Bomb Group had sponsored. General Eaker had decided that new bomb groups and individual crews coming from the States needed indoctrination and orientation on emergency procedures in the United Kingdom as well as an introduction to barrage balloons, escape and evasion, air-sea rescue, and a realistic introduction to air warfare.

The 92nd Bomb Group moved in early January 1943 to Alconbury Airdrome near Huntington, Bedfordshire, leaving about a third of its personnel behind to run the 1/11th Combat Crew Replacement Training unit. Most of those who stayed at Bovingdon were those trying to evade combat, including two squadron commanders, one a West Pointer. The 92nd had also sent twenty-five navigators to North Africa, using B-25s to guide fighter groups there and to navigate C-47s with paratroopers on the initial invasion. The 92nd had also traded all of its new B-17Fs to the 97th Bomb Group, in exchange for their old B-17E models prior to the 97th group's participation in Operation Torch. Thus, the 92nd ranks were decimated, and it would be three months before it could return to combat. It was during these three months that I continued to try to make B-17 copilots out of the Royal Air Force transferees.

Sometime in February 1943, Maj. William Wyler arrived straight from Hollywood at our station with a group of cameramen experienced in aerial photography. All of them were commissioned officers and, being ten to fifteen years our senior, they were all first lieutenants and captains. I was intrigued with these people because they had shot the movie *Wings* with Clara Bow and most all of the other popular airplane movies that had inspired me and gotten me interested in joining the Air Corps.

Capt. Tom Hulings and I were assigned to fly for them, and we began immediately to experiment with manned camera stations all over the airplane. We set one up in the radio room hatch, with the camera on an installed tripod and the cameraman's head and shoulders outside the airplane. Other photographers were set up in the nose, tail, waist gun and ball turret positions.

After preparing these camera positions, we flew several orientation flights to give our cameramen an opportunity to adjust to their tasks of photography from an aerial platform. We then flew to Bassingbourne, the home field of the 91st Bomb Group, near Huntington, where we met with American pilots coming into the U.S. Army Air Corps from the American Eagle Squadrons and several members of the newly formed 4th Fighter Group.

One of the new RCAF transferees who had been assigned to the USAAC 4th Fighter Group was Flight Officer Willard Milliken, whom I would get to know in the postwar Air National Guard, and who would later attain the rank of brigadier general and commander of the fighter wing of the District of Columbia Air National Guard. Another was Lt. Joe Egan, of the famous 56th Fighter Group, whom I later roomed with en route home for a thirty-day leave.

After several meetings and briefings, we finally took off, climbed to about nine thousand feet, where six of our P-47s began making fake combat gunnery passes at us. Their maneuvers were from all quarters, both high and low, while we cruised as slowly as possible so that the cameramen, especially the one whose head and shoulders were outside the airplane, could get good shots. These films turned out to be excellent footage, and we were told that they would be used to help train aerial gunners. About a month later I saw some of these shots on the Pathe News in a London movie theater, shown as actual aerial combat over Germany!

Major Wyler later placed a movie camera in every bomber in the 8th Air Force, so that the various crewmembers could photograph most of the aerial action. He ended up with copies of thousands of feet of combat film from which he later made the movies *Twelve O'Clock High, Memphis Belle,* and others. Recently, while watching the remake of *Memphis Belle,* I again saw some of those shots of P-47s making passes at us, some combat actions shot from our group, the 92nd, and lots more from other 8th Air Force groups. The credit at the end of the movie listed "With the cooperation of Mrs. William Wyler," who apparently still has possession of these films.

After arriving in Bovingdon in August of 1942, we were issued bicycles as our only means of transportation. They were fine for traveling around the air base, but not adequate to go to Watford, Maidenhead, and other desirable points, particularly if one consumed a few "pints." By chance I met an Englishman who had a motorcycle for sale. It was an Enfield and perfect for personal transportation. He said he could not get petrol for it, and I purchased it for sixty-five pounds. I, of course, operated it on aviation fuel, and our 100–octane aviation fuel made it really scramble. As far as I knew, I was the only second lieutenant in England with my own personal transport vehicle, and I visited all the pubs far and wide, even hoisting it into the bomb bay of a B-17 and taking it along on a trip to Scotland.

One evening while returning home, I rounded a curve a little too fast and hit some loose gravel on the road. The centrifugal force slid the bike out from under me and threw me into a thick holly hedgerow. I awakened a few minutes later on the porch of an adjacent house with a man gently plucking the holly thorns out of me. He turned out to be Dr. Isaac M. Jones, chief medic of Scotland Yard and a very influential Londoner. He and Mrs. Jones lived in Portland Place, in London's West End, but they also owned this country house near my airdrome at Bovingdon, Herts. Their country home had been built in 1400, and the ceilings were only about six feet high, with huge hand-hewn beams supporting them. Dr. and Mrs. Jones were both Australians, and they had traveled all over the world. He told me he'd even once visited my hometown of Charleston, West Virginia, and had attended a meeting of coal companies. Later, in 1956, I called them and planned to visit them while on an Air Force inspection trip. Sadly, Dr. Jones died suddenly, while I was on my way to England. My visit with Mrs. Jones was, of course, much saddened by his death.

By April 1943, the USO had begun sending entertainers to visit the American forces in Europe. Bob Hope came with Frances Langford, Merle Oberon with Adolphe Menjou, and Mitzi Mayfair with her dancers. I had the pleasure of having lunch with Hope. He never stopped telling jokes, none of which, if I could remember them, would be printable here!

By now spring weather made English living a little easier. I was rooming with Lt. Alec Hogan, of Starkeville, Mississippi, who was also a flying school classmate. Our duties at Bovingdon were boring, and we both had pangs of conscience because our group was preparing to go back on operations at Alconbury. Most of our classmates were getting ready to fight the "Hun," and we both felt like 4-Fers and slackers. We both agreed that it was time to join them.

We asked for transfers back to the 92nd, but Alec somehow was sent to the 95th Bomb Group, which had just arrived from the States. Unfortunately, he was shot down on April 13, 1944, en route to Berlin. He survived to become a prisoner of the Germans. My transfer back to my old outfit, the 92nd Bomb Group, came through as requested.

6

![US Army Air Forces star insignia]

1943

On January 4, 1943, the 92nd Bomb Group was ordered to move to Alconbury Airdrome, just north of Huntington. It left behind members of the 325th Squadron plus several additional personnel to continue training replacement crews from the States. Its organization, the 1/11th Combat Crew Replacement Center, was commanded by Maj. John P. Dwyer.

By early May the group had received orders to resume combat status, and at the same time Col. Jim Sutton, its commander, was transferred to a North Ireland modification depot. His transfer was rumored to be due to insubordination toward his superior officers, particularly Brig. Gen. Ira Eaker, 8th Air Force bomber commander. It was also said that he'd been charged with a security violation involving a lady friend. He was replaced by Lt. Col. Bascombe R. Lawrence, executive officer of the 91st Bomb Group.

About this same time several new B-17 groups began arriving in England, and the 1/11th Combat Crew Training Center at Bovingdon was hopelessly swamped. The 8th Air Force ordered each new group to move in with an existing group and train with their host group. The 95th Bomb Group moved into Alconbury in early May and began flying and training with the 92nd.

During this period, every facility was crowded, which required the double-parking of airplanes on the parking cul-de-sacs (hardstands). On the evening of May 27, while the ordinance crews were loading five hundred–pound bombs on the airplanes in preparation for a mission the next day, a B-17 of the 95th Bomb Group blew up, shattering the entire airdrome. Nineteen men were killed instantly and over thirty more were injured. Four B-17s were damaged beyond repair and a dozen more were also damaged. In one instance, an engine blown off an airplane hit a B-17 on its free fall back to earth, breaking the B-17's fuselage in two pieces at the waist-gunner's position. The group's new commander, Lt. Col. William M. "Darky" Reid, was seated in group operations, near the flight line, talking by phone to the 1st Air Division headquarters when the explosion took place. The concussion from the blast blew him and his chair into the room behind him! He was not seriously injured.

This tragic accident was the worst of its kind in the 8th Air Force. Small pieces of human flesh remained stuck to trees and fences for weeks afterward.

My transfer to my old group occurred just as the 95th Bomb Group was departing for its new base at Framlingham in East Anglia. It would become a member of the new 3rd Division of the 8th Air Force. I was welcomed with open arms upon my return to my old squadron, as was Colonel Reid, who had been my original squadron commander. During the winter months of 1942–1943, when several crews and especially navigators had been on temporary duty in support of the North African operations, many of the remaining 92nd Group crews had been sent as replacements to the 91st, 303rd, 305th, 379th, and 306th Bomb Groups. These five groups had continued operations against Nazi submarine pens, harbors, and coastal airfields after the 97th, 301st, and 93rd Bomb Groups had left for North Africa in October 1942, and their ranks had been decimated by German fighters and antiaircraft (flak) guns.

Maj. Jim Griffith of Kingsport, Tennessee, had been promoted to commander of the 407th Squadron, replacing Lt. Col. Bob Keck, who had returned to the States to bring back a squadron of special B-17s known as the YB-40s. They were the results of efforts by Capt. Robert "Pencilbutt" Reed of the 92nd group, who had gone back to Wright Field, Dayton, Ohio, in the fall of 1942 and had engineered additional turrets and guns to give each bomber formation added firepower. He added a twin .50-caliber turret over the radio room, a new twin .50-caliber turret on the nose, and twin .50s at each waist and tail position, plus an extra fuel tank in the bomb bay to give the airplane a greater range. The YB-40 could not carry bombs, because all of the extra turrets, guns, and ammunition increased its total weight to the maximum for takeoff (about sixty-five thousand pounds). As I recall, we carried about eight thousand rounds of .50-caliber ammunition on each YB-40, each round weighing more than half a pound. This added ammunition and the weight of the additional turrets and guns made the airplane difficult to handle at high altitudes and barely flyable if even one engine was lost.

After a checkout ride by Capt. Don Parker to make sure I could handle a B-17, I was assigned a crew, consisting of Lt. Don True of Texas, copilot, and what was left of the crew that had been with Lt. Col. Bob Keck when we flew the Lille, France, raid the previous October.

My first mission of 1943 was flown as copilot on the new YB-40. We were sent to the 305th Bomb Group to escort them, much like an escort destroyer in the navy, as they flew to bomb the submarine pens at St. Nazaire on the coast of France. The 305th Group was a sister group in our 40th Combat Wing, as was the 306th Group at Thurleigh.

The 305th was commanded by Lt. Col. Curtis E. LeMay, who would later command the new 3rd Air Division, then the B-29s of the Pacific Air Force, the peacetime Strategic Air Command, and who one day would become chief of staff of the U.S. Air Force. To his credit, he was by far the most knowledgeable on bomber tactics of all the senior officers in the 8th Air Force. In his younger days he'd been a bombardier instructor and had also taught navigation, while most of the other commanders and general officers had been flying pursuit aircraft and practicing World War I tactics. Thus, he had a much better understanding of what was necessary to assemble the bombers and find and hit a target. Though he was the most junior of all senior officers, his grasp of and his solutions to the problems facing the 8th Air Force in those early days were soon recognized. And, though he was never given full credit at that time, he developed the system we employed throughout the war to assemble our groups at altitude above the weather using low-frequency radio beacons, then fly a zigzag route from one beacon to another to pick up our sister groups and thus form the bomber train in the sky while en route across the English Channel. Along with Col. Frank Armstrong (of the 306th), he also developed the concept of keeping bombers in tight "combat box" formations, with lead, high, and low groups forming the "box." Keeping the bomber groups and wings in close formation was a must if our fighter escort was to be able to cover us properly and give us adequate protection from German fighter airplanes.

I'd never met Colonel LeMay before that morning, but I was impressed by the meticulous and thorough way he conducted his briefings. He was all business and made certain that everyone understood every detail. (His nickname, used with discretion among members of the 305th, was "Iron Ass.")

The mission was uneventful except for some accurate flak over the target. We did not lose any airplanes, but it was easy to see that the YB-40 idea was not practicable. The airplane was so heavy that we had to use additional power to stay in formation, and the addition of six or seven extra guns to the 298 total already in the eighteen airplanes of a regular group formation had little if any effect. Our group continued to fly them through the months of June and July but then retired the YB-40 from further service.

Our living quarters at Alconbury left a lot to be desired. None of the squadron's living quarters were at the base. All were dispersed, and I was quartered in a large frame building called Upton House about three miles north of the base, along what was called the Great North Road, said to have been built by the Romans. There were about fifty of us there, and our only recreations were volleyball, poker, and Nora's Pub.

Among our regulars at poker was Capt. "Father" Eddie Seward, our Catholic chaplain, who was the nightly winner and who always said the Lord made him do it, because he gave all his winnings to the Church. Ten years later, after several martinis at my friend Vincent Reishman's home one night, I learned that Reishman and Seward had been roommates at Notre Dame. In the alcoholic enthusiasm of our discovery we decided to arouse the (by then) Monsignor Seward, of the Cleveland Diocese, from bed to relate our discovery. It was 2 A.M., and to say the least he was less than delighted to hear from us.

Nora's Pub was a different story. Nora's was a small roadside pub that served mostly the farm folks who lived nearby. Her allotment of spirits was very small, and when we arrived we drank her dry every night. This, of course, left her old customers with no bitters or gin, and Nora became exceedingly frustrated with us.

We soon all got together, chipped in a few pounds each, and sent an airplane to a Scottish distillery. It returned with forty cases of scotch whiskey and fifty cases of beer and ale. We promptly gave Nora a dozen cases of the scotch and twenty cases of beer. We never again had a complaint from Nora or any of her regular local customers.

Living in Upton House presented another problem for me. I roomed with Capt. Frank Ward in an upstairs bedroom. We were losing lots of crewmen in combat and thus losing and gaining roommates almost daily. I recall seeing seven .45-caliber pistols piled in the corner of one room as personal effects left from officers who had been shot down. We were all certain that we'd be shot down, and the constant apprehension of what the next raid would bring made it difficult to sleep. One such night I awakened and smelled smoke. I turned over and saw a lit cigarette in the bed next to me. The thought immediately went through my mind that if the Jerries didn't get me, Ward would burn me up in Upton House.

On May 23, 1943, Lt. Col. William "Darky" Reid of Columbus, Georgia, became the commander of the 92nd Bomb Group. He was the second member of the group I'd met when I joined it back on April 30, 1942, upon graduation from flight school. He'd briefly been my squadron commander, was promoted to group operations officer, and went on to become the group executive officer prior to our departure for England. All of these rapid promotions came about because of his seniority.

Darky Reid had graduated from Air Corps Flying School in 1933. He then served in a pursuit squadron commanded by Capt. Budd Peaslee. He left active duty in 1935 because the U.S. government could not pay him. As he explained it to me, each commander in those days drew from the finance officer each month the funds in cash needed to pay all the members of his command. This system continued until after World War II. It seems the government did not have enough money to meet all the pay requirements, so they simply gave the commanders the amount they could afford for that particular month, or about 80 percent of that needed. His commander would then pay himself and the squadron flight leaders their full pay and apportion the remainder to the second lieutenants, who ended up with a fraction of their normal pay. After a few months of this, Reid found a job with the fledgling Eastern Airlines and left active duty, becoming an Air Corps reserve officer on inactive duty.

In 1937, as the military buildup began, he was recalled to active duty, and thus by Pearl Harbor he had been a commissioned flying officer for seven years and on active duty for more than five years, making him a very senior officer among the thousands coming on duty for the war. He went from first lieutenant when I first met him to lieutenant colonel in the three months before our departure for England. A year later he would become a full colonel.

Darky Reid was a great commander because he was an outstanding aviator, affable and easy to know, had a great sense of humor, and was too compassionate to suit the West Point generals, some of whom were simply out to further Gen. "Billy Mitchell's cause"—the theory of precision daylight bombing—as I would so well learn in the months to come. While some commanders avoided flying combat missions, Darky Reid did not hesitate to lead our group and soon established a routine of combat leaders in which the commander, the executive officer, the group operations officer and his assistant, and the four-squadron commanders took turns leading our group. The only exception was when our group was scheduled to lead the 1st Air Division or the entire 8th Air Force, in which instance Colonel Reid would go as air commander in the lead airplane.

June of 1943 saw the true beginning of the strategic air war against Germany. A sufficient number of new bomb groups had arrived from the States to form the 2nd and 3rd Air Divisions. The 2nd Air Division was made up largely of B-24 groups, and the 3rd Air Division, like our 1st Air Division, was composed entirely of B-17s. These totaled about thirty-six bomb groups, each initially containing thirty-six airplanes, for a total of about thirteen hundred bombers. As airplane production back home grew, the size of these groups increased from thirty-six to nearly one hundred airplanes each by D-Day, 1944, providing more than three thousand heavy bombers in the 8th Air Force alone. The 15th Air Force, based in Italy, had nearly two thousand more by the fall of 1944. All of this was in addition to the B-26 medium bombers, plus over a thousand fighter airplanes.

Our first American escort fighters also joined us in June 1943. The 56th Fighter Group, flying P-47s, began operations, and the

members of the three American Eagle squadrons of the RAF transferred to the U.S. Army Air Corps and formed the 4th Fighter
Group. It too was equipped with P-47s and, as I recall, British Spitfires. Additional fighter groups soon joined us with their P-38s,
and finally, by late 1943, the first P-51 Mustangs arrived.

Our first escorted mission was one to Huls, Germany, on
June 22, 1943. It was the first effort by the 56th Fighter Group.
While our bombers were cruising along the route at twenty-five
thousand feet, Col. Hubert "Hub" Zemke brought his fighters
over us at about thirty-two thousand feet, the P-47 being by far
the best high-altitude fighter airplane in the war. Suddenly, the
German fighters appeared and began attacking us, with our P-47s
circling overhead as if they did not know what to do. The following day we held a critique with the fighter pilots and told them to
either get into the fight or go on back to the States. From that day
on, they attacked with vigor. The only problems were that there
weren't enough of them and they did not have the range to take
us into Germany. The Luftwaffe soon learned this and just held
off their attacks until our escort had to leave. Then all hell would
break loose.

As we began pressing our bombing attacks deeper into Germany without fighter escort, our losses grew to unbearable
heights. Official loss reports often did not cover those aircraft that
ditched in the English Channel and the North Sea and many more
that crash landed at various airfields all over England. It became
obvious that we had to have longer-range fighters to protect our
bombers en route and while over the target areas. At the same
time the RAF was saying, "We told you daylight bombing was
not feasible, now come join us on the night raids." Of course, this
rankled our Air Corps generals, who were out to prove Billy
Mitchell's theory of precision daylight target bombing versus the
British nighttime area bombing system being advocated by Air
Marshall Sir Arthur "Bomber" Harris.

At one point in July of 1943, we apparently came very close

to performing night raids. We were ordered to start night practice missions and to install covers on our superchargers, which glowed like lanterns when they became white-hot during use in flight. I flew one such practice mission and, on my second one, stuck my airplane in the mud when the left main gear dropped off the taxi strip as I taxied out for take off. Obviously, someone at the top changed his mind, for we never again heard about night operations. As I look back now, I feel it was unfortunate that we didn't give night bombing a try, because the B-17 was a good high-altitude airplane. It's exhaust-type superchargers provided plenty of power at high altitude. None of the German fighters were effective above thirty thousand feet, and I always felt that our losses might have been minimal.

During May and June of 1943, I was still a member of my old 407th Bomb Squadron. The squadron commander was now Maj. Jim Griffith, who had replaced Lt. Col. Bob Keck. Keck, who had gone back to the States and led the YB-40s back to our group, had then moved on to become commander of the 327th Bomb Squadron.

Jim Griffith was probably the best squadron commander and the best air commander in the group. He was a quiet, efficient, hardworking officer with higher morals and more character than any I knew. He successfully led many raids and was an officer whom every other officer and every enlisted man respected. After the war, he had a long and successful career with Eastman Kodak. I have had several enjoyable visits with him in recent years.

Early in July 1943 I was transferred to the 326th Squadron and was assigned as a flight leader. Lt. Augustus Claude "Gus" Ahrenholtz, of New York City, a YB-40 pilot, became my copilot, Lt. Henry A. "Harry" Hughes of Jersey City my navigator, and Lt. Edward T. "ETO" O'Grady of Staten Island, New York, my bombardier. All were class people, courageous in combat, and all had successful careers after the war. Gus was an automobile dealer in Middletown, New York; Harry became the national sales manager of St. Regis Paper; and Eddie O'Grady became a chemicals salesman in New York.

One of our first raids together was to bomb the tire plant in Hanover, Germany, on July 17. Our group was leading the 8th Air Force, and Lt. Col. Willie Buck was our air commander. The 407th Squadron was leading our group, and I was leading my squadron (the 326th) as the high squadron. Lt. Hoot Gibson came along as my copilot, as it was his last (twenty-fifth) mission and he felt our position as high squadron lead would be a safe place to complete his last combat flight. It was customary to let officers pick their last missions.

All went well, and we were cruising along at twenty-six thousand feet leading the bomber train over Holland, heading for Hanover. The sky was clear and we could see for miles. Suddenly, we received a recall message, and Colonel Buck signaled all of us to prepare for a 180–degree turn, to return to England. As we executed our turn, all of the other groups behind us did likewise, leaving us at the tail end of the bomber train and perhaps three to four miles behind the group, now in front of us. Immediately, out of the blue, thirty to forty German fighters headed straight into us in frontal attacks, one wave after another, their cannon fire looking like headlights on their wings blinking at us. The first wave hit our group's lead airplane, temporarily stunning the pilot and wounding Colonel Buck. A brightly burning oxygen fire spurted from the side of his plane, and we could see the crew scrambling in the cockpit to control the plane and fight the fire. My high squadron flew on the left side of the lead squadron, which left it to my copilot to fly our airplane, since he was on the side of our airplane next to the leader and had a better view of the leader's actions.

We had one of William Wyler's 16mm movie cameras on top of our cockpit dashboard and, as I sat there aghast with fear, watching the fighters shooting at us, Hoot Gibson called to me to take some pictures. I grabbed the camera and began rolling the film. When it ran down I began winding it as I continued to take pictures. A few moments later I heard Gibson chuckling over the interphone. I had wound the camera so intently that I'd caused the entire side of the case to come loose—screws were dropping onto the floor and the camera was literally coming apart. I was so scared I hadn't realized what I was doing, as I actually twisted the camera into two pieces. We landed safely, and Hoot Gibson finished his twenty-five missions. As fate would have it, he was later killed flying in the States. Lieutenant Colonel Buck was awarded the Distinguished Service Cross for his leadership that day, and Capt. Don Parker, lead pilot of the mission, was awarded the Distinguished Flying Cross.

A week later my group again led the 8th to Hanover, with Major Griffith as air commander. We destroyed the tire plant known as the Kontinental Gummiwerke A.G. Waren, Walderstrasse. The story was best told by Lt. Keith Koske, the navigator of the crew of Robert Campbell of my squadron:

"We were on our way into the enemy coast when we were attacked by a group of FW-190s. On their first pass, I thought sure they had hit us, for there was a terrific explosion overhead, and the ship rocked badly. A second later the top turret gunner, S/Sgt. Tyre C. Weaver, fell through the hatch and slumped to the floor at the rear of my nose compartment. When I got to him I saw that his left arm had been blown off at the shoulder and he was a mass of blood. I first tried to inject some morphine, but the needle was bent and I could not get it in.

"As things turned out it was best I didn't give him any morphine. My first thought was to try and stop his loss of blood. I tried to apply a tourniquet, but it was impossible as his arm was off too close to his shoulder. I knew he had to have the right kind of medical treatment as soon as possible, and we had almost four hours of flying time ahead of us, so there was no alternative. I opened the escape hatch and adjusted his chute for him.

"After I adjusted his chute and placed the ripcord ring firmly in his right hand, he must have became excited and pulled the cord, opening the pilot chute in the updraft. I managed to gather it together and tuck it under his right arm, got him into a crouched position with his legs through the hatch, made certain again that his good arm was holding the chute folds, and toppled him out into space. I learned sometime later from our ball turret gunner, Sgt. James L. Ford, that the chute opened okay. We were at 24,500 feet about twenty-five miles due west of Hanover, and our only hope was that he would be found and given medical attention immediately.

"The bombardier, 2nd Lt. Asa J. Irwin, had been busy with the nose guns, and when I got back up into the nose, he was getting ready to toggle [release] his bombs. The target area was a mass of smoke, and we added our contribution. After we dropped our bombs, we were kept busy with the nose guns. However, all our attacks were coming from the tail. I tried to use my interphone several times but could get no answer. The last I remember hearing over it was shortly after the first attack, when someone was complaining about not getting any oxygen. Except for what I thought to be some violent evasive action we seemed to be flying okay.

"It was two hours later when we were fifteen minutes out from the enemy coast that I decided to go up and check with the pilot and have a look around. I found the pilot, Lieutenant Campbell, slumped down in his seat, a mass of blood, the back of his head blown off. This had happened two hours before, on the first attack.

"A shell had entered from the right side, crossed in the front of F/O Morgan, the copilot, and had hit Campbell in the head. Morgan was flying the plane with one hand, holding the half-dead pilot with the other hand, and he had been doing it for over two hours.

"Morgan told me we had to get Campbell out of his seat, as the plane couldn't be landed from the copilot's seat as the glass on that side was shattered so badly you could hardly see out. Morgan and I struggled for thirty minutes getting the fatally injured pilot out of his seat and down into the rear of the navigator's compartment, where the bombardier held him from slipping out of the open hatch. Morgan was operating the controls with one hand and helping me handle the pilot with the other."

Questioned as to why he had not received help from other crewmen, Lieutenant Koske explained that the men in the rear of the aircraft were unconscious from the lack of oxygen, the air lines having been shattered several hours before. The ship had been undefended save for the nose and ball turret guns. Morgan's feat had been little short of miraculous. He had kept the ship in formation and, holding the fatally wounded pilot off the controls with one hand, had flown to the target and out again alone and unaided, with no radio, no interphone, and no hydraulic fluid. The ship was brought safely home for an emergency landing on the coast.

The other crew members were T/Sgt. John A McClure, S/Sgt. John E. Foley, Sgts. James L. Ford, Reece B. Walton, and Eugene F. Ponte.

Since I did not participate in that raid, I was dispatched to pick up F/O Morgan and the remainder of his crew and bring them back to Alconbury. To this day I remember walking up the fuselage to the belly hatch under the cockpit, where Tyre Weaver had bailed out and where Lt. Bob Campbell had died. The recessed walkway was a pool of blood about one-inch deep, reaching from the navigator's compartment to the bomb bay bulkhead. We removed all personal belongings from the damaged airplane and soon flew back to our home base.

In early December 1943 the War Department awarded now 2nd. Lt. John C. Morgan the Congressional Medal of Honor. Lt. Gen. Ira C. Eaker made the presentation, which was broadcast over the BBC. Lieutenant Morgan recounted this memorable mission of 26 July 1943. The following March, he was shot down on the first raid to Berlin and spent the next fourteen months as a prisoner of war. He later joined the Texaco Oil Company, where he enjoyed a long and successful career as an aviation representative.

About the same time, we learned that S/Sgt. Tyre Weaver had been picked up by the Germans, had been hospitalized, had recovered, and was being repatriated. Three months later he stopped by his old squadron to say goodbye on his way home. He returned to his home in Alabama, where he served many years as a deputy assessor of his county.

The character and strength of the enemy opposition on the Hanover Raid was additionally illustrated. Seven aircraft sustained battle damage; Capt. Blair G. Belongia was forced to ditch in the English Channel; S/Sgt. Etheridge Lamm, top turret gunner of Lt. Ralph Bruce's crew, was killed instantly, just before the initial bombing point, by a bullet which came in from above; the aircraft piloted by 1st Lt. Alan E. Hermance was last seen to hit the water about ten minutes off the island of Nordernay, with one engine on fire and the tail chewed up.

Captain Belongia's aircraft, after having sustained an attack by seven FW-190s just after entering the coast, suffered the loss of two engines and lagged behind the formation. Bombs were salvoed south of Hanover, the ship was put into a slow shallow dive, and the shortest route was taken for home, with every possible care taken to avoid the heavily defended areas. However, flak was encountered at Ashendorf, and to avoid it the aircraft dropped down to fifty feet above the ground, narrowly missing some of the town's buildings. Heavy fire was encountered over Emden Bay, but the enemy smoke screen helped immeasurably. Limping along over the sea at above two hundred feet, the aircraft was attacked by an Me-109. Captain Belongia dropped down to above twenty-five feet, and the fighter, unable to dive under the ship, nosed up to the right, where S/Sgt. Joseph M. Walsh, the tail gunner, fired a burst into its belly. The Me-109 crashed into the sea.

With fuel running low, Captain Belongia ordered that everything removable be jettisoned. Over the English Coast the number one engine went dry. When no suitable landing field was sighted, Captain Belongia turned the aircraft back out to sea and ordered the crew to take their position for ditching. The plane was brought down on the water about two miles from shore near Sharingham; the crew abandoned ship safely and piled into one dinghy. An hour later they were picked up by a fishing boat and landed on their own coast.

7

Pete's Story

Pete Edris, of Jersey City, New Jersey, had bunked next to me in flying school, and we had become good friends. He was transferred to the 306th Bomb Group at the end of 1942 while I was in North Africa. He was shot down in March 1943 and evaded capture for some time. As such, he was reported as having been killed in action.

His father had been an insurance agent in New Jersey and had purchased a sizable life insurance policy on young Pete's life, when Pete was at an early age. Life Insurance contracts prior to World War II did not contain war loss exclusions, so the company paid his mother, as his beneficiary, the full sum of the policy. His mother, being a good American citizen and doing everything possible to help the government, promptly purchased U.S. Government War Bonds, which paid 3 percent interest, with her insurance settlement money. A few months later the Germans found Pete and sent him to a prisoner of war camp, Stalag Luft III. His mother was then notified that he was not dead but instead a prisoner of war. She then had to return the insurance money and, to do so, she borrowed the full sum from a local bank—at 6 percent interest. After the war, when Pete asked her why she didn't cash the bonds to pay back the insurance company and save all that extra interest, she replied, "Oh I just couldn't do that to our country in the midst of this horrid war." But here is Pete's story in his own words:

"On December 31, 1942, I was transferred from the 92nd Bomb Group, 325th Bomb Squadron, based at Bovingdon, England, to the 306th Bomb Group, 369th "Fighting Biting" Bomb Squadron, based at Thurleigh, England. I had the distinction of being transferred into the 306th at the same time that General (then Colonel) Armstrong took command of the Group. Gen. Frank Armstrong, a native North Carolinian, was said to be the general portrayed by Gregory Peck in the movie *Twelve O'Clock High.*

"I was made an aircraft commander before I left the 92nd, and my made-up crew was just as inexperienced as I was. I tell you, it was scary and depressing. I was leaving all my friends and classmates, heading out to a strange place in a strange left seat. It was a low point, but not nearly as low as it was going to get in just a few more months.

"Luckily for everyone concerned, my squadron commander, Major Terry, told me his procedure for a replacement crew was to give an experienced copilot (ten missions) my command, and I was to take his position as copilot for ten missions. Then I would get my own crew. Good idea! The only thing wrong with this procedure was I would be copilot for 1st Lt. "Rip" Riordan. Well, that really scared the devil out of me, because I had been reading in the *Stars & Stripes* about his escapades, bringing back B-17s all shot up, engines out, stabilizers shot off, holes all over the place. Plus, I found out quickly that he was very *gung ho* for flying missions to completions—no abortions, period. He wouldn't even take the two days a month we got off to go to London. He might miss a mission.

"First chance we got, we went out to the airplane, *WaHoo Mark II.* I said, 'What happened to *Mark I?*' I shouldn't have asked. He brought it back from Romily sur Seine on two engines, all torn up. It never flew again. It was cannibalized and used for spare parts. When I got in the copilot seat, I immediately noticed a big round hole, filled smooth, in the rudder pedal. 'What's that?' 'Oh, that's where a 20mm went through the pedal. Luckily, the copilot had his foot on the rudder bar at the time.' Hot dog! I wanted to go home! In retrospect, it was a good thing to be with him. He had crammed a lot of experience into a few missions.

"We flew eight missions together, starting January 13, 1943. We worked out a neat plan to fly the airplane in formation. If you remember, it handled like a truck at twenty-five thousand feet. Well, he handled the stick and rudder. I handled the throttles, prop pitch, cowl flaps, flaps, landing gear, and everything else I could get my hands on, in case of overrunning the formation when some slob leading up front changed his air speed by one knot. Believe me, I used them all one day when we were flying in a position called 'filling in the diamond.' We flew directly behind the flight leader and a little bit below his prop wash. When the FWs came in at 12 o'clock, you flew prop wash. When they came in at 1 o'clock, you flew echelon on the number three man. When the flack came up, we would drop back a few feet and do our own evasive action (for purposes of morale only, of course).

"We were in this position on the bomb run. We started to overrun the flight leader, coming right under his belly. I looked up through the little window in the roof and could see five 1,000–pound bombs through the open bay doors, which were going to be released in about thirty seconds. Remember, you couldn't chop the throttles off: you had to pull them back slowly on account of the waste gates from the superchargers would slam shut, and you could overspeed your engines. Well, off come the throttles, cowl flaps open, props to flat pitch. Still overshooting. Down come the flaps, down come the gear. Uh, oh. We've stopped. Up comes the gear, flaps up, close the cowl flaps, advance the throttles, prop pitch back to normal—busier than the proverbial one-armed paperhanger! I wasn't scared; I was working too hard.

"My fateful day was rapidly approaching. March 6, 1943, we had a mission to Lorient, France—sub pens, I believe. We barely made it back to Exeter in southern England—I mean, the whole group. We were all out of gas. That's another story.

"Anyway, we spent the night in Exeter. Accommodations were so bad, I couldn't sleep. The next day, March 7, we flew home to Thurleigh. The navigator and bombardier and I went into Bedford Key Club and had a party, and we got to our barracks about midnight. There was a mission the next morning, and I wasn't supposed to go because a ranking officer was checking 'Rip' out to lead. Well, I didn't want to get behind in missions, so I told operations I'd go along as an extra gunner in the nose. I was qualified as a gunner. 'No,' they said. Some 'gravel agitator' was picking his own five missions (milk runs) to get an Air Medal. He was flying as an extra gunner. He was not qualified as a gunner, nor was he qualified on high-altitude oxygen use.

"At three in the morning (three hours sleep), Rip awakened me and said, 'Come on down to the briefing anyway.' I said, 'No, @%#*!! If I can't go the way I was trained, I'm not going.' But he talked me into it. I got dressed.

"8:22 P.M.—the mission was to the marshaling yards at Rennes, France. What was I doing at this briefing? I wasn't going. When the briefing was over, someone called my name and asked if I wanted to fly with a crew in another squadron whose copilot was sick. Didn't have to go! Well, I violated the first rule you learn in the service: 'Don't volunteer for anything.' I volunteered. A little side note of history here. Our Squadron, the 369th, went from March 8, 1943, through forty-seven missions without a loss! Incredible! Me and my big mouth!

"I met Rip in the locker room getting dressed for the mission. I remember telling him I had a funny feeling I wasn't coming back on this one. Strange.

"I was with Lt. Otto Buddenbaum and his crew, and we took off at dawn. Going across the channel, we discovered that the number two and number three engines were not producing enough power. It was difficult to stay in formation. And guess what our position was? Last plane, last group, out of four groups. Purple heart corner! We debated aborting, but decided against it.

"As soon as we crossed the French coast, one FW sneaked in on us from six o'clock, no less! Bam, Bam, Bam! Three 20mm rounds with instant fusing hit us—one in each wing, severing the aileron cables, and one in the top turret. We immediately lost our position and protection from the formation and were all alone. We used rudder to keep the ship right side up. When she would go into an uncontrolled bank, we would both push top rudder, which would slew the bottom wing forward, more lift, and up she'd come, only to dip over to the other side. Buddenbaum told everyone to bail out. I ripped off my mask and hollered, 'Let's see if we can turn it around and dive it for home.' Well, about this time, most of the gunners were gone, and this FW began having a field day—another six o'clock high pass. The armor plate behind our seats saved us. It stopped bullets, but the rest of the shrapnel came between the seats—down the aisle, so to speak, and blew out all our instruments and cut off the throttle handles. Our number three engine was now burning like crazy—all flames, no smoke. It was a mess.

"The FW then came up and flew on our right wing for a few seconds. I guess he wanted to see what was holding us up. He was so close I could see his drooling fangs, his square, black goggles, and swastika tattooed on his left cheek. Ha, ha! Just like the propaganda pictures! I said to myself, it was time to go. I went out the nose hatch, counted to ten, and pulled the ripcord. Guess we were around twenty-two thousand feet by then. I know it took about thirty minutes to come down. It was the only mission I forgot to leave my wallet in operations. So, on the way down, I took it out and tore up all the incriminating evidence, like old football stubs and licenses. I saved Doris's picture and nine British pounds I had in my wallet.

"The chute opened with such a jerk it sprained my back, and my left boot and shoe flew off, and my escape kit flew out of my leg pocket. I reached down and took my right boot off and put in on my left foot to keep it a little warmer. It was cold. I estimated I was at twenty thousand feet by then, and it was maybe forty below zero. It was quiet—dead quiet. I made a standup landing on my right foot. With no shoe on the left one, I figured I might break it. I was shaking so badly I had to sit down.

"I landed in a farmer's front yard, and the chute draped over an apple tree. The French farm people came running to help me. Believe it or not, I still had the ripcord; I had stuffed it in my pocket. Funny how you remember the little things. In the States, if you don't bring back the ripcord, drinks are on you at the club, so the story goes.

"Well, anyway, the women got the chute disposed of quickly—all that silk. About this time someone hollered, 'Allemande!' (Germans!) Well, my little crowd disappeared, except for one chubby fellow who quickly put me in a pigsty with a bunch of pigs. A truck full of German soldiers came into the farm and looked around. When the coast was clear, the French farmers put me in a little abandoned chicken coop out in the field, gave me some wine and bread and hard-boiled eggs. I stayed there until dusk. I was then escorted to the farmhouse, which was full of peasants, gawking and giggling and shaking my hand. I took off my flying clothes and put on a sweater and civilian pants and a pair of slippers and was introduced to a Frenchman, Henri Du Fretay. He was dressed in a business suit and came from St. Brieux, about thirty miles away. Remember now—no sleep, the night of the 6th, three hours on the 7th, and we walked most of the thirty miles the night of the 8th. I was tired, to say the least, when we reached his apartment in St. Brieux just after dawn on March 9. I slept all day, and that evening I was taken across town to another family. Their names were Madame Dinton and Jeanne-Lou Dinton, her daughter. I stayed three days in their home, hidden in the attic.

"The sweater the farmers gave me I found to be full of fleas, and I was bitten severely. Madame Dinton would come to my hiding place and massage my back, as it was hurting especially after walking thirty miles that first night. She washed the sweater for me also.

"An interesting little side note here. I had my 'air force' on—a gold ring—and Madame Dinton said I had to take it off because it would be too conspicuous. The Germans took all of the French rings and melted them down for their war effort. So she took my ring and buried it in a tin can, along with my nine pounds, in her back yard. Well, in 1946, when I was back at Duke University, I wrote to them and was immediately sent my ring with an explanation why they couldn't send it to me before—because nobody in the military occupation forces apparently felt like helping her. But, anyway, I got my ring back, and I still wear it today.

"After three days, a former French pilot came to me, to be my guide out to the country again. His name is Eric Delval, and he brought two bicycles. We pedaled all day, passed many German soldiers along the way, and arrived at a Catholic parish in Lamballe, France. Luckily we were only a hundred yards from the house when I got a flat tire on my bicycle. This was approximately March 13. I stayed here two weeks with a French priest named Monsieur L'Abbe Corbel and his maid, Mary. He spoke a little English, and my French was improving. We got along well. He even broke out a bottle of cognac he was saving for the 'Liberation.' We finished it.

"After the two weeks at Lamballe, another priest came, and we bicycled to Dinan. This was about March 27. Dinan is a fairly large city, at the base of the Brittany Peninsula. I spent one night with a family, and it was here I was introduced to Dr. Jacques Cooicou and a Spanish man, who was the janitor of the building where Jacques had his apartment in Paris. We left the next morning, March 28, on a train for Paris, a ten-hour ride. Jacques had brought me travel papers from Paris, given to him by the Prefect of Police of Paris, Monsieur Boussiere. My papers said I was a

Czech slave laborer named Bumbroski and I was deaf and dumb, and that Jacques was taking me to Paris for an operation. I had to act like I was deaf and dumb for ten hours on the train. It was like flying five missions all at once. We got to Paris in the evening and went by subway to his apartment at 1 Rue de Lord Byron, just off the Champs-Élysée. I met Jacques' wife, Suzanne, and their maid. This was a five-story building, and they lived on the top floor.

"I spent approximately six nervous weeks there. We were told in England not to stay in any one place too long, so I kept needling Jacques to get me on my way. He kept saying he had to be very careful whom he contacted. I could appreciate that.

"One day he told me he had found an American woman, caught in Paris by the war, who was eight months pregnant. She was with the Underground and would be by to interview me later. Her name was Madame Feldon. And I feel, in retrospect, she possibly was the one who informed on me. She came by and asked how long I had been in France. I said, about nine weeks. She said that was way too long. They would take me back out to the tip of the Brittany Peninsula, and I would be flown back to England at night in a Lysander (a British highwing monoplane that can make short field landings and takeoffs). Then she asked if I would like to take back some military information with me. 'Sure,' I said. 'No papers. I'll memorize everything.' She told me how the Germans were transporting submarines by railroad in pieces to the French coast ports of St. Nazaire and Lorient. She gave me the bomb damage on the raid to Fennes, March 8. Boy, how this information I was willingly collecting came to haunt me in the next few days.

"She left, and two days later, May 15, 1943, the Gestapo broke open the door of the apartment and arrested me, Jacques, Suzanne, and the maid. We were all handcuffed, taken in the elevator to the waiting van, and driven to La Fresnay Prison, just outside Paris.

"Here I was put in solitary confinement for seventy-seven days and told repeatedly that I was to be shot as a spy and saboteur! I was in civilian clothes, no dog tags (I never wore them), carrying in my head all kinds of enemy information, fed to me by what I think was a German secret agent. I didn't have a leg to stand on. Being convinced I was to be shot, it was here that I learned how fear can be a physical pain. I was fed a piece of bread a day with watery soup, full of bugs and worms. This was bad! The seventy-seven days with the Gestapo were worse than the two years with the Luftwaffe. The bed being infested, I was again attacked by fleas. At one point, I counted over five hundred bites from my waist down. Knowing I was going to die, I started to pray. I felt like a hypocrite, a drowning man clutching at a straw, so to speak, but I went ahead and prayed anyway.

"One morning, after having beseeched the Lord twice a day for weeks and having nothing seem to happen, I looked up at the ceiling and said, 'If you don't get me out of here, to hell with you!' That afternoon they took me out of my cell for interrogation at Gestapo headquarters in Paris. Interrogations were the beginning of eventual release to the Luftwaffe, I found later. See, they knew who I was. They didn't want me to know that they knew it—better to beat information from me. I told this part of my story to my minister of our community church in Syosset, New York, thirty years ago. His remark was, 'You were in a state of grace.' You know, you can go through your whole life hearing words you don't know the meaning of, and 'grace' was one of them. I didn't want to show my ignorance, so I didn't ask what he meant. But as soon as I got home, I looked it up. The religious definition says, 'The unmerited divine assistance given man for his regeneration of sanctification.' Of course, it could have been sheer coincidence, too. I choose to accept the first explanation.

"At Gestapo headquarters, I was interrogated for four hours. Now I know all about the training we had back in the States, where they taught us to give our name, rank, and serial number only and don't try to outsmart the interrogator. He's smarter than you are. Don't get cute. Just give your name, rank, and serial number. But I was being interrogated as a spy, and by the Gestapo. If I had given them my name, rank, and serial number, I would have gone right back to the 'hole.' I gave this guy a story, which I had practiced in my cell for hours before. It was a story as near the truth as possible without giving away any names of persons or places. He accepted it. He was so dumb I thought it was a trap. He was not an experienced interrogator. He even gave me half of his sandwich and a cigarette. I remember in his room there was a full-length mirror. I got a look at myself, and I was a mess. I guess I lost about thirty pounds, long greasy hair, scraggly beard.

"I was released from La Fresnay Prison about a week later, on about July 29, 1943, and put in the hands of the Luftwaffe. Then on to Frankfurt am Main, Germany, where DuLag Luft was located. This was a transient camp where I stayed about five days. Here we were given a military interrogation. I didn't tell them anything either. Well, I'd been down for months, so there was nothing I could tell them. Next was on to Stalag Luft III, Sagan, Germany, where I arrived around August 5. I remained in the camp until January 1945, when we were forced to march westward—ten thousand American and British flying officers. The Russians were thirty kilometers away, to the east. We marched west about eighty kilometers in three days and nights in temperatures around ten to fifteen degrees Fahrenheit. It was on this march that both my hands and feet were frostbitten. We were later put on boxcars and taken to southern Germany, fifty men to a boxcar. We were jammed together, many were sick, and they let us out once a day for water and to relieve ourselves. Those four days were awful. We ended up at Mooseburg, Germany, where we were liberated April 29, 1945, by Patton's 3rd Army, 14th Army Division.

"My stay in Stalag Luft III is another story entirely. Two interesting sidelights: (1) I was one of the twenty-four servicemen during World War II who were reported killed in action and later turned up alive. I was officially dead for approximately two months. I was also one of the few servicemen who had a medal taken away from him. I was awarded the Purple Heart posthumously, and approximately two months later, when I turned up alive, my mother had to give it back. (2) The day we were shot down, one of our waist gunners, 'Mo' Moriarity, landed with his parachute about a mile from me, and he was back in England in twenty-three days. He wrote a book. It's quite a story!

"One last comment: I learned that a person can take a great deal more punishment than he thinks he can, and with no lasting ill effects. I wouldn't take a million dollars for the experience, but I wouldn't do it again for a million."

Pete spent more than two long years as a prisoner of war. In June of 1945 I was stationed at Avon Park Army Air Base, Florida, and Pete suddenly showed up next door at the Sebring Army Air Base. I had just been detailed to lead a nine-squadron air show around the country, and I invited Pete to come along for the next scheduled show in Detroit, where Gen. Tooey Spaatz was speaking at a big war bond rally. When we arrived at the air base in Detroit, at what is now Detroit Metro International Airport, we saw hundreds of German prisoners working at the base. Some were helping maintain our Air Force planes. Pete was of small stature, lean and wiry, and at times impulsive. As we walked through one of the hangars we passed a group of German prisoners squatting in a circle, talking in German, of course. As we passed them, Pete suddenly turned and kicked one of the prisoners in the rear, knocking him on his face in the floor, and began lecturing the group in German. I grabbed him and pulled him back, but he kept right on poking his finger at the group and yelling at them. I asked him what in the world he was doing. He said, "I'll not ever again let any Kriegie son of a bitch call me an SOB!" To say the least, the German prisoners were in shock.

Pete later became an American Airlines pilot, and back in the mid-1960s he used to fly through my hometown of Charleston, West Virginia. At this time I had an aviation business at the airport, and Pete would stop and visit during his forty-five-minute layover. One day he invited me to see his brand new Boeing 727, and I sat in the cockpit until takeoff time as he explained all the latest gadgets to me. In the meantime, I had told him I was a candidate for the local County Court and, as I departed and walked through the airplane to descend the rear stairway, Pete came on the cabin speaker saying to the passengers, now largely local Charleston people, "Ladies and Gentlemen, my friend Mr. Kemp McLaughlin, now walking through the cabin, is a candidate for the County Court of your county, and I do hope you'll all vote for him." A loud round of laughter ensued as I disembarked, red-faced.

8

Schweinfurt and Stuttgart

In late July 1943, Maj. Bob Eaton arrived at our station with a group of new aircrews fresh from the States. We welcomed them, for our ranks had been thinned from combat losses, and we greatly needed them.

Major Eaton had been with the 19th Bomb Group, a B-17 group in the South Pacific, when the war began and had flown raids with them in the months following Pearl Harbor. Along with Capt. Colin Kelly and others, he had been awarded a chest full of medals, as they were the only Heavy Bomb Group there in the early days and made the headlines sinking ships and rescuing General MacArthur and his staff. They rarely had the heavily defended targets and concentrated numbers of enemy fighters that we faced in Europe.

After he had delivered his new crews, he decided an Air Medal from the European Theater would look good on his record for the future, so he asked Colonel Reid if he could stay a few days and fly five raids with us, thus qualifying for an Air Medal. Colonel Reid approved his request, and he was assigned to my crew for our next raid. On July 29, I was ordered to lead a twelve-ship group to the German port of Kiel. Our target was the shipyard, which was heavily defended with antiaircraft guns and some very large 225mm naval guns.

We got off without mishap, formed up, and found our position just above and behind the lead wing with almost perfect timing, all due to Harry Hughes's excellent navigation, which kept me at the right positions at the right times. Major Eaton was standing between the pilots, just behind our seats, where he could see all the action.

All went well so long as we were over the North Sea, but as we neared the coast just north of the Frisian Islands the German fighters began attacking the groups ahead of us. As we neared the Initial Point, where we were to begin our bomb run, the flak guns opened up on us. We were fourth in line to bomb, so the air was black with smoke from all the shots before us, and new puffs were exploding all around. Suddenly the larger naval guns let go, creating huge explosions directly on our course to the target. The gunfire rocked the ship and made terrifying sounds as the shrapnel rattled against the sides of our plane. Some of the explosions were so close that they were fiery red instead of black, but on the bomb run itself we could not deviate from course as the bombardier took control and steadied his sights on the target.

After bombs away we were soon back out in the North Sea, away from the flak and fighters. The German fighter pilots seldom attacked us out at sea, because if shot down they could not survive in the cold North Sea waters.

Except for a few wounded, we made the trip back to base without mishap. We landed and taxied to our parking revetment (hardstand) with Major Eaton still standing in the cockpit. Upon shutting down the engines the crew disembarked, but I as usual had to complete the airplane Form 1a and enter any write-ups of things that needed to be done to have the airplane ready for its next flight. All of this took six or seven minutes, and when I stepped from the airplane I looked forward to talking with Major Eaton about our flight. He was nowhere to be found. I later learned that he had changed his mind about flying any more missions with our group and had left immediately for London.

Fifteen years later, after I had been turned down once for promotion and Eaton had become a major general, my old friend Lt. Gen. Ernest C. "Moose" Hardin told me that General Eaton had become upset with me because I had turned down a commission in the Regular Air Force and that he had placed a letter in my personnel file denying me any further promotion as a Reserve officer.

In the ensuing months of 1943, I flew on raids from Norway to Switzerland along with all my squadron mates. So much has been written about aerial combat and the strategic bombing of Europe in World War II that there is little I can add at this date. However, some of the unusual things that happened to me and my crewmates and those of my friends in combat, as well as a few noteworthy incidents and personalities encountered, are worth relating.

Those of us who went to England in 1942 and 1943 encountered some difficult problems. None of us, of course, had any aerial combat experience, and we had no idea of what we were to do. Looking back on our situation, I now realize that our leaders didn't either. A big problem of fighting in the air is that at twenty-five thousand feet there is no place to hide. Every bomber raid into Europe was an airborne repetition of the "Charge of the Light Brigade," for the flak and fighter attacks were almost continuous along the overland portion of the route to the target and back.

We were also attacking the Germans over their homeland. If we shot up their airplanes, they could simply bail out and hitchhike home. If they shot us up, and we were lucky enough to limp away from the Continent, we still had to make it back across the North Sea or the English Channel, where for most of the year the water was too cold for human survival. In addition to our combat problems, none of us had any experience in instrument or bad-weather flying, and England was perpetually overcast, rainy, and foggy. We were more often than not flying in low ceilings, with only a half to two miles of visibility. There were no instrument-approach or radar-approach systems, and we had to grope through the fog to find our home base, where Very pistol flares were being fired like large roman candles to help us find the end of the runway. Because our bases were so close together, this crowding led to several tragic aerial collisions while forming up, in which as many as six or eight airplanes collided and crashed at one time. Of course, these were not reported as mission losses.

"Blitz Week," in July 1943, consisted of aggressive penetration of Germany by the 8th Air Force, with losses that were to foreshadow the raids on Schweinfurt. After six missions in seven days, the 8th Air Force had lost a hundred planes. That meant one thousand men were dead, missing, or captured.

Most of my friends and flying classmates were shot down during that terrible summer of 1943. Losses became so great and morale so low that often, if word got out of an impending raid, some of the enlisted crewmen would get lost and not be around at mission briefing time.

Official combat loss rates reported by 8th Bomber Command were growing. From August to December 1942, only 2 percent of the aircraft were lost per mission, and from January to June 1943, the figure was 6.6 percent lost. From July to December 1943 the rate rose to 9.1 percent, a figure which, air crews quickly realized, meant that mathematically they would not survive beyond eleven missions!

By August 1943 we were attacking German targets on a steady basis. My group flew eight missions that month, dispatching 152 airplanes and losing eight. On August 17, the anniversary of the first 8th Air Force bombing mission, we were briefed to attack the ball bearing factories at the town of Schweinfurt, deep in Germany.

Eighth Air Force Bomber Command had a plan for the target that, had it been carried out properly, would surely have cut our losses. The plan was to have the 3rd Bombardment Division (under Air Commander Curtis LeMay) lead the bomber sky train to Regensburg and bomb the aircraft factory. Our 1st Bombardment Division was to follow directly behind them (no more than fifteen to twenty minutes behind), then turn and bomb Schweinfurt as the 3rd proceeded on farther east to Regensburg. After Regensburg they were to turn south and fly to North Africa, while our 1st Division would turn west and return to England. The 2nd Division B-24s were to fly a diversionary mission up the North Sea and attack a target well north of us. Thus, the German fighter defenses would be split apart and unable to determine and anticipate just what our routes would be.

But the timing of the departures for the three divisions, and their arrival over their respective targets, would be critical. And, just as with the raid on the Ploesti refinery, we couldn't carry it out as planned and our losses were enormous.

We were alerted and briefed for takeoff at about 0800 hours, but the weather in our 1st Division area was zero-zero. Visibility was so bad one could not even see to taxi an airplane: we couldn't even get the airplane to the end of the takeoff runway.

The weather was better in 2nd and 3rd Division areas, so Bomber Command decided to send them on and let us follow later. I recall sitting on the ramp beside my airplane with my crew for *three hours* waiting for the takeoff signal. Sgt. Bob Johnson was a new radio operator assigned to me for the mission. He'd been on some rough missions, and his regular crew, led by Capt. Hans Johnson, had been shot down on August 12 while he was grounded for medical reasons.

Like all of us, he was scared to death and began pacing the ramp, saying aloud that he was certain that we'd get it that day. I finally had to make him sit down and be quiet while I gave the crew a pep talk on how we were going to come through in fine shape.

At last we got the signal to go. We climbed aboard, started the engines, and began to taxi. It was now almost 11 A.M. and the other divisions were nearing their targets, with the German fighters attacking them all the way.

We got off and formed our wing formations and proceeded on our routes without our escorts, as they had not had time to return from their earlier escort flights with the 3rd Division, get refueled, and become airborne again. By noon we were entering the Continent, and the western European-based German fighters had had just enough time to land, refuel, and rise to meet us. Our losses were heavy. I was leading the high squadron in the high group, just about the safest position in the entire wing. We saw lots of fighters, and many attacked us. Flak was heavy over the target area, and we hit heavy propeller wash from the groups ahead of us in the bomb run, which rocked the airplane, making things difficult for the bombardier and our wingman, who had to stay in close formation for the bomb drop.

After bombs away we turned for home. As we flew out of the heavy flak area around the target, here came the German fighters for more. But again my high squadron was not hit hard. I do remember that en route home a German Heinkel 111 (a bomber, fitted out with a rocket on each wing) came straight on, right down the line of our formation, not more than twenty feet above us. No one got a shot at him, because he came and went so fast that no one saw him until it was too late. He was one gutsy daredevil.

Our escort fighters met us on the way out and helped us limp home. The 8th Air Force reported the loss of sixty bombers that day, but there were probably a hundred lost. My group lost one aircraft to fighter attacks just before reaching the target, and Capt. Roland Sergeant and crew were shot down on the way home. To make things worse, we did little damage to the target, which meant we would have to go back again.

During July and August of 1943, a new facet of bombardment was begun in the 325th Squadron of our group. It was to be known as H2X and was in fact the mounting of a very large and crude radar in the radio room of the B-17. From that position the radar operator could see through the clouds to guide the navigator and pilot along the route and tell the bombardier when to release the bombs.

This system had been developed by the British for their night bombing raids, where navigation was understandably difficult. American proponents of daylight bombing were forced to admit that weather conditions in Europe often prevented the use of the Norden bombsight. Several technicians arrived to help train our people to operate and maintain the equipment.

The first raids using this equipment were difficult because the radar units were so unreliable. More often than not we'd go to targets covered by clouds and the equipment would fail before we could get there. We'd then have to go to a secondary target or drop on any target we could find. This was the beginning of the end of daylight precision bombing, for radar and other means of "blind bombing" could not be considered precise for many years to come.

At first our 325th Squadron would send one of its radar-equipped B-17s to the group scheduled to lead the 1st or the 3rd Division, and the Division Command pilot of the group would fly in the copilot's seat of the radar bomber, leading our Air Division from that position. As we gained more radar-equipped airplanes, we'd furnish one to each wing leader and finally to each group. In time, each group was given its own radar-equipped B-17s, and our former 325th Squadron became the 382nd Bomb Group and served as a research and training station for blind bombing techniques.

Our group had given birth to the 1/11th Combat Crew Replacement Center at Bovingdon and now had produced the new radar bombing organization at Alconbury. All of this occurred in the first year we'd been in England and all while helping carry the fight to the enemy. We were soon to move on to a new station, to give the new radar bombing group room to grow.

Late in August 1943, I received orders promoting me to captain. I had survived seventeen missions and gotten a pay raise too. It wasn't all bad. Besides, at that point I thought being a captain in the U.S. Army Air Corps was the greatest thing that could happen to a twenty-four-year-old. I quickly wrote my sweetheart at the University of Arkansas and told her I could now afford to marry her.

On September 6, we were briefed for a raid on Stuttgart, Germany. My crew had been selected as a "lead crew," a new concept designed to get the most experienced personnel in the lead airplane, in an effort to get more bombs on the target.

Maj. McGehee Word had become our squadron commander, and he flew in the copilot's seat as the group air commander. Our takeoff and formation assembly over our assigned low-frequency radio beacon were uneventful, and we departed Control Point 1 without mishap. Just after we entered the Continent we began to get fighter attacks, and Lt. Asher—flying on my left wing—called for permission to pull out of the formation to check a smoke problem in his bomb bay. He slid to his left about three hundred feet and all seemed to be okay, when suddenly his airplane blew up in midair. Large chunks of airplane and engines went hurtling through the sky, leaving several parachute canopies floating through the air like autumn leaves, with nothing hooked to them. They were the parachute bundles that the crewmen had laid beside their gunnery positions and never had a chance to put on. It was a sickening sight, because we all knew that the poor devils were falling to earth without a chance to survive, a scene that we'd see many more times.

Col. Bob Travis, a very senior Air Corps officer, popular with Bomber Command generals, was the 1st Bombardment Division air commander for this mission. The wing with which he was leading the division had recently been equipped with the latest long-range B-17s, and his airplanes carried 2,750 gallons of fuel, enough for seventeen hours of flight. Our airplanes carried only 1,780 gallons of fuel, enough for nine to ten hours. When Colonel

Travis's wing arrived at the Initial Point to begin their bomb run from a point south of the city, he discovered the route into the city was covered with clouds, but the area east of the city was clear. He immediately chose a new Initial Point about forty miles east of the city and ordered all of us to follow him eastward, then turn west on the bomb run.

A very large turning radius is required to turn a large wing formation of airplanes, and each group must have room to position itself to ready its formation for its bomb run. We were the third wing in line, and our route extension to the east and back again required almost an extra hour of flying time. To top it all off, when we did approach the city from the east the clouds had moved east also, and we had no chance to bomb our primary target. Heading west from Stuttgart, Major Word picked Strasbourg as our secondary target, and we dropped our bombs on it as briefed. En route home across France we realized that we were going to run short of fuel. I called our squadron leaders and told them I was reducing power to fourteen hundred revolutions per minute and would make a one hundred-foot-per-minute descent toward the English Channel. Major Word told them not to try to stay in close formation, as luckily there were no enemy fighters around at that time, but to try to keep up in a large gaggle in case we should encounter fighters again.

From the time we passed Paris on to the English Channel there developed one of the most pitiful scenes of the entire war. Crewmen were tossing out guns, ammo belts, and everything else they could find to lighten their airplanes. Airplane commanders were calling their group leaders, saying they were running out of fuel. Others were announcing that they were bailing out or would crash land in France. Everywhere below me I could see airplanes descending toward the green fields of western France.

As we reached the English Channel, Major Word gave our airplane commanders permission to seek any airfield and land as quickly as possible. At mid-Channel my red lights came on, denoting that I had only a few minutes of fuel left, and I began to tense because I could not yet see England, let alone a place to land. As we approached the White Cliffs of Dover I could see two airplanes circling and felt there must be an airfield there. When I'd gotten closer I saw a large sod RAF field, and the two B-17s circling were trying to call the control tower. They obviously hadn't been around long enough to become streetwise, or they'd have already landed.

As soon as I saw the field I dropped my landing gear and flaps and headed in for a landing. Going down the final approach I could see the two airplanes that had been circling heading in from different directions for landings and at least a dozen more coming in from all different headings. After landing, as I rolled to the far side of the field I was certain there would be landing collisions near the center of the field. But as I turned to taxi toward the control tower airplanes were landing in all directions, passing each other without mishap. The gods were with us again.

We parked our airplane near the control tower and started up the steps to send a message to our base, to let them know what had happened. When we were about halfway up the steps this short but sturdily built colonel passed us. He dashed up to the controller and with a thick Pennsylvania Dutch accent yelled, "For God's sake, call Air Sea Rescue, my whole bomb group is floating out there in the Channel!" He was Col. Budd J. Peaslee, commander of the 384th Bomb Group. His group had been in England only about sixty days, and he'd lost them all in the "drink" that day.

I would soon get to know Colonel Budd really well, because shortly thereafter Col. Bob Travis ironically gave his group command to Col. Dale Smith and transferred Colonel Budd to the position of deputy wing commander of our 40th Combat Wing, which consisted of my 92nd Bomb Group and the 305th and 306th Bomb Groups. But Colonel Budd's airplanes weren't the only ones in the Channel that day. Colonel Travis's decision to lengthen the route caused more than two hundred airplanes to run short of fuel. Many crashed or crash landed in France, and an untold number ditched in the Channel. No figures on airplanes lost were ever published for that raid, but I'm sure we lost a hundred or more B-17s that day. My own group lost three airplanes on this raid, including Lieutenant Asher's. The other two ran out of fuel and were abandoned over France.

At the Air Division critique two days later, Colonel Travis simply said, "I didn't know that the other wings didn't have long-range airplanes." The old "C'est le guerre" attitude prevailed, and we heard no further explanation of Travis's error. He later was promoted to major general and was killed in a B-29 crash at what later became Travis Air Force Base in California.

9

Assembling
"The Mighty Eighth"

Lt. Col. Leslie Lennox was a pilot in the 95th Bomb Group and best describes our procedures in getting our bombers together for a raid:

"Of all the stories that have been written and movies that have been shown about the 8th Air Force, very little attention has been given to what was involved in assembling twelve hundred B-17s and B-24s each day, getting them in formation to carry out a strike against Germany. Certainly showing bombers under attack by fighters, or encountering heavy flak, was a reality, and is interesting to watch. Also, stories about some of the rougher missions make for interesting reading. But what was going on over England, each morning, could get just as scary to the crews as the time spent over some of the targets. The planning and coordination that had to be accomplished during the night by the operations planners of each group so that the crews could be briefed was unbelievable. If the planners had failed to do their jobs properly, the skies over England would have been a free-for-all among bomb groups.

"The rendezvous points, altitude, and times had to be precise and known by all the crews before the 8th Air Force could get in formation. The success of the planners in accomplishing their mission enabled the 8th Air Force to become the most powerful air armada ever assembled. In my view, how this was accomplished is one of the major untold stories of the war.

"I was a pilot in the 95th Bomb Group, and what follows is a typical mission from a crew member perspective, as I remember it:

"Early in the evening, our Squadron Operations would post the names of the crews that were scheduled to fly the following day. There were two ways we could be notified if the group had been alerted to fly. One was by means of lights on the front of the orderly room, and the other was the raising of colored flags. If a green light was on, the group was alerted; if a red light was on, we would fly; and if a white light was on, the group would stand down. The light was monitored frequently throughout the evening to learn our status. Normally, we would know before going to bed if we would be flying the next day.

"On the morning of a mission, the CQ (charge of quarters) would awaken the crews about four or five o'clock, depending on takeoff time. The questions we always asked were, 'What is the fuel load?' and 'What is the bomb load?' If he said, 'Full Tokyo tanks,' we knew we were going into Germany. Shortly after we were awakened, 6-by-6 trucks would start shuttling us to the mess hall. We were fortunate always to have all the fresh eggs we could eat when flying a mission. After breakfast, the trucks carried us to the briefing room. All of the crew members attended the main briefing, and then the navigators, bombardiers, and radio operators went to a specialized briefing. At the main briefing, in addition to the target information, antiaircraft guns, fighter escort, and route in, we received a sheet showing our location in the formation, the call signs for the day, and all information we would need to assemble our group and get in the bomber stream.

"After briefing we got into flight gear, drew our parachutes, and loaded onto the trucks for a ride to our plane. We were now guided by the time on our daily briefing sheet. We started engines at a given time and watched for the airplane with which we would be flying in formation to taxi past, then we would taxi behind him. We were following strict radio silence.

"We were now parked nose to tail around the perimeter, on both sides of the active runway and extremely vulnerable to a fighter strafing attack. At the designated takeoff time, a green flare would be fired and takeoff would begin. Every thirty seconds an airplane started takeoff roll. We were lined up on the perimeter, so the twelve airplanes of the high squadron would take off first, followed by the lead and then the low squadron.

"Each group had a pattern for its airplanes to fly during its climb to assembly altitude. Some would fly a triangle, some a rectangle, and our group flew a circle, using a "Buncher" (a low frequency radio station) that was located on our base. The patterns for each group fit together like a jigsaw puzzle. Unfortunately, strong winds aloft would destroy the integrity of the patterns, and there was considerable overrunning of each other's pattern.

"I flew during the winter of 1944 and 1945, and many of our takeoffs were made before daylight. It was not uncommon to climb through several thousand feet of cloud overcast. Also, it was not uncommon to experience one or two near misses while climbing through the clouds, although you would never see the other airplane. You knew you had just had a near miss when suddenly the airplane would shake violently as it hit the prop wash of another plane. It was a wonderful feeling to break out on top where you could watch for other planes and keep from running into one another. To add to the congestion that we were creating, the Royal Air Force Lancasters, Halifaxes, and Wimpys would be returning from their night mission and would fly through our formations. Needless to say, pilots had to keep their heads on a swivel and their eyes looking out of the cockpit.

"After takeoff, the squadron lead would fire a flare every thirty seconds so that we could keep him located and get ourselves into formation quicker. The color of our group flare was red-green. The first thing you would see, when breaking out of the clouds, was a sky filled with pyrotechnics. Now you had to search the sky for the group flare, which would identify the lead airplane of your squadron. Once you had it located, you could adjust your pattern to climb more quickly into formation with him. As each airplane pulled into formation, they would also fire a flare with the lead plane, which then made it much easier for the following aircraft to keep him in sight. I think most crew members would probably agree that the pyrotechnic show in the skies over England when the 8th was assembling was a rare sight to behold.

"The order of progression for assembling the 8th Air Force was first to assemble the flight elements, then the squadrons, the groups, the combat wings, the divisions, and, finally, the Air Force.

"As soon as the four squadron elements were formed, the high, low, and second elements would take up their positions on the lead element to form a squadron. When the three squadrons had completed assembly, it was necessary to get into group formation. This was accomplished by having the three squadrons arrive over a preselected fix at a precise time and heading. The high and low squadrons were separated by one thousand feet and, after getting into group formation, would maintain their positions by following the lead squadron.

"It was now necessary to get into the combat wing formation. We were in the 13th Combat Wing, which consisted of three bomb groups: the 95th, the 100th, and the 390th. Whichever group was leading the wing that day would arrive over a preselected point at a precise time and heading. Thirty seconds later, the second group would pass that fix, followed by the third group thirty seconds after that. We were now in combat wing formation. The navigators in the lead airplane had a tremendous responsibility to ensure that the rendezvous times were strictly adhered to.

"There were three divisions in the 8th Air Force: the 1st, 2nd, and 3rd. The 1st and 3rd consisted of B-17s only and the 2nd of B-24s. The B-24s were faster than the B-17s, but the B-17s could fly higher. Therefore the two were not compatible in formation. As a result, the 1st and 3rd would fly together, and the 2nd would fly separately.

"Now that the groups were flying in combat wing formation, it was necessary to assemble the divisions. This was usually accomplished at the 'coast-out' fix, a city on the coast selected as the departure-point fix. The group leader in each combat wing knew his assigned position in the division and the precise time that he should arrive at the coast-out departure point in order to assume that position. The lead group in the division that had been selected to lead the 8th on the mission would be first over the departure fix. Thirty seconds after the last group in the first wing passed that point, the second wing would fall in trail, and so on until all combat wings were flying in trail, and the division was formed. One minute later, the lead group in the other division would fly over that point, and the combat wings in that division would follow the same procedure to get in formation. When all of its combat wings were in trail, the 8th Air Force's B-17 strike force was formed and on its way to the target. At the same time the 2nd Division's B-24s were assembling in a similar manner and departing to their target.

"A major problem that presented itself on each mission was the bomber stream's getting too stretched out. It was not uncommon for the headlines in stateside newspapers, in trying to show the strength of our Air Force, to state how the first group of bombers were bombing Berlin while the last group was still over the English Channel. It made great headlines but was an undesirable situation. It meant that the groups were out of position and were not keeping the proper separation. Furthermore, it was almost impossible to catch up and get back in the desired formation. This made the entire bomber stream more vulnerable to fighter attacks.

"Finally, our planners figured out what we were doing

wrong. When the first group departed the coast-out fix, it started its climb to what would be the bombing altitude. Then, as each succeeding group departed that fix, it too would start climbing. The problem with this procedure was that as soon as the first group started its climb, its true airspeed would start to increase and it would encounter different wind velocities. Now it would pull away from the group in the back of it, and the stretching of the bomber stream would begin. By the time the last group would be leveled off, with a true airspeed approaching 250 miles per hour, the bomb stream would be really stretching out.

"The solution to this problem that had been frustrating the bomber crews for so long was pretty simple. We would no longer start climbing at the coast out, but instead, at a designated time, all groups would start climbing, irrespective of position. This meant that we all would have similar true airspeeds and be influenced by the same winds aloft. That took care of that problem. It was still possible for a group to be out of position because of poor timing, but the entire bomber stream wouldn't get all stretched out.

"When you consider the way our air traffic control system operates today, and all the facilities at their disposal to guide each individual airplane through the sky to ensure its safety, it's almost unbelievable that we were able to do what we did. To think of launching hundreds of airplanes—in a small airspace, many times in total darkness, loaded with bombs, with complete radio silence and no control from the ground—and doing it successfully, with minimum experience, is absolutely mind-boggling.

"The accomplishments of the 8th Air Force will be reviewed by historians from now on. There will never be another air armada to compare. I feel confident they will never cease to be amazed at our ability to assemble hundreds of heavy bombers, under the conditions we were faced with, into the devastating strike force we now fondly refer to as 'The Mighty Eighth.'"

In the meantime, our fighter escort groups of P-47s, P-51s,

P-38s, and RAF Spitfires, all of whom were based along the East Anglia coastal areas, were on their outbound routes and altitudes from the English Coast into the Continent. Their takeoff times were set to enable them to join us at the point of entering the Continent and to cover us as far as their fuel would permit.

As more fighter aircraft became available and long-range fuel tanks began to stretch their operational areas, 8th Fighter Command began a relay system in which one group of escorts would relieve the previous group and take us on to the target area. After a fighter group would finish its escort duty, it would usually hit the deck and strafe any targets available en route home.

10

Schweinfurt Again

We had attacked the ball bearing works in Schweinfurt on August 17 but had failed to hit our targets with enough bombs to do any real damage, and the cost in planes lost was terrible. As the leader of my squadron, I'd luckily had a pretty easy flight that mission while the rest of the bomber force was losing sixty bombers to the enemy, plus all those that crash-landed in England.

We all knew that we'd be going back to this target, and each of us hoped he'd not be selected for that raid. No such luck. After the second Schweinfurt raid, known later as "Black Thursday," one of the news people asked my crew to write our story of what actually happened. Capt. Harry Hughes, my navigator, Capt. Eddie O'Grady, my bombardier, and I wrote the following story, which was published in *True Magazine* in 1944.

"The day before the second Schweinfurt raid our group was alerted earlier than usual. As was our daily custom, we strolled over to the weather office to ascertain which of the target areas was most favorable. This habit of 'checking the weather' is one to which most air crews are addicted, mostly because one can predict fairly accurately from the target areas just how difficult the coming raid will be.

"The weather maps showed a front lying over England, and Capt. R.F. Kernan, the base meteorologist, predicted that the following day it would be affecting the English Channel and adjacent land areas both in England and on the Continent. The most favorable target area was deep in the heart of Germany. This section was under the influence of a high-pressure system that gave promise of clear, cloudless weather. However, continued poor weather over our base areas made it seem highly improbable that we could take off the next day.

"As we walked back to our quarters to dress for the evening mess, we stopped at Group Operations. In the Air Corps, Group Operations was equivalent to the managers' offices in a private corporation, and all the orders from higher headquarters came there, where they were in turn transmitted into orders for the various squadrons.

"Since the squadron navigator usually helped prepare the flight plans for the mission, he was not scheduled to fly on that mission. Colonel Brousseau, our group operations officer, unthinkingly asked my navigator, Capt. Harry Hughes, if he was working that night; then remembering, he smiled and said, 'Oh, no, you are really working tomorrow.' He too had checked the weather and realized that if we went out the following day, it would probably be a long, hard trip. He then told us that we were to lead the group the next day.

"On every raid, one of the group executive officers flew in the lead ship; so I asked Colonel Brousseau if he was going with us. He said no, that since we were scheduled to lead the air division, one of the executive officers from our Combat Wing Headquarters would ride with us as the air commander.

"At dinner and in the club that night, many of the officers were hazarding guesses as to the target, for their curiosity had been aroused because of the unusually early alert. After dinner, we relaxed in the club lounge, which was a large Nisson hut with two stoves, a radio, and some chairs. We started a bridge game to pass the time but soon broke it up in favor of a good night's sleep, an absolute necessity for anyone in combat.

"We retired to our respective quarters not knowing at what hour we would be awakened. We went to bed but not to sleep, for the weight of the responsibility that we would have tomorrow was not conducive to peace of mind. I turned in early and in what seemed like thirty minutes was awakened by our C.Q., who informed me that breakfast was at 5 A.M. and briefing at 6 A.M. The weather at Podington, England [our new base, to which the 92nd had been moved, from Alconbury, the week of September 11] on that morning of October 14, 1943, could only be described as zero-zero: no visibility and no discernible ceiling, a typical English fall morning—heavy fog and drizzle.

"After breakfast, 6 by 6 trucks transported us all to Group Intelligence for the mission briefing. The pilots, navigators, and bombardiers were briefed in one room, while the gunners and radio operators were briefed in another.

"The first thing my crew looked for, as did others, was the number of antiaircraft batteries that were positioned within reach of our route and the target area. Bomber Command usually tried to use routes that avoided heavily defended points, but there were targets in areas like the Ruhr Valley that could not be reached without flying through heavy flak. Another important item to every bomber pilot was the distance from the enemy coast to the target—for flying through gunfire was one thing, but if one lost an engine with a long distance to go, his chances were very slim of making it back to the English Channel. It was an accepted maxim in the European Theater of Operations that 'he who is not in formation, is *not*.' As a group leader, I would often slow my air speed as much as ten miles per hour to give other ships that were having engine trouble a chance to stay in the protection of the formation.

"After all the officers had arrived, the doors were locked and Major Harmon, our Group Intelligence Officer, began the briefing by pointing out the importance of the target and emphasizing the fact that the ball bearing production facilities at Schweinfurt produced 75 percent of all ball bearings being used in the German war effort. If the target was destroyed he said, 'It would be of incalculable value to both us and the Russians. The production of everything that moves on wheels would be severely handicapped.'

"'Secret: Send in Clear.' The teletype message read at all 8th Air Force briefings for Mission 115 to Schweinfurt, Germany, on October 14, 1943, is remembered by many. Unfortunately, many men lost more than their memory on Black Thursday. There has been speculation that the Germans knew that a very important effort was 'going down' that day, even before 8th Air Force crews were aware of it. Of course, there were many security leaks, but it would be interesting to know if the 'Send in Clear' means it could have been tapped from a telephone line leading into any of the many U.S. bases in England. We know that the Luftwaffe had time to call fighter support from all over the Reich and occupied countries for the day's event. That message read:

SECRET: SEND IN CLEAR AUTH. COL. WALLACE 8 BC 0 - 853 - E. TO ALL LEADERS AND COMBAT CREWS. TO BE READ AT BRIEFING.

THIS AIR OPERATION TODAY IS THE MOST IMPORTANT AIR OPERATION YET CONDUCTED IN THIS WAR. THE TARGET MUST BE DESTROYED. IT IS OF VITAL IMPORTANCE TO THE ENEMY. YOUR FRIENDS AND COMRADES THAT HAVE BEEN LOST AND THAT WILL BE LOST TODAY ARE DEPENDING ON YOU. THEIR SACRIFICE MUST NOT BE IN VAIN. GOOD LUCK, GOOD BOMBING.

"Everyone was impressed with the importance of the target, but we were all anxiously waiting his description of the route and the amount of fighter escort we would have. As you can understand, any good combat officer is ready to go to whatever target may be assigned him, but the old law of self-preservation always comes into play, and he has to think not only of his own life but also those of his crew whose safety is in his hands.

"Intelligence explained that our route would be east over the English coastal town of Felixstowe, across the Channel into Holland, on into Germany, thence south of the Ruhr to the target. P-47 Thunderbolts would join us at the Dutch Coast and escort us to the Ruhr Valley, then again meet us northeast of Paris on our more southern route home. Only light flak was anticipated along the route, and approximately three hundred eighty 75mm and 90mm antiaircraft guns firing twelve bursts per minute were in the target area. That computes out to well over fifty thousand shells being fired at every formation from the IP (Initial Point) through the target run. But the most staggering piece of information given us that morning was that there were seven hundred single-engine and four hundred twin-engine enemy fighter aircraft within eighty-five miles of our route. This more than anything brought home to us the danger of the flight ahead of us.

"Pictures of the target area were flashed on the screen, and we were able to study an enlargement of the largest factory building in detail. Next, Capt. Raphael Kernan gave us a detailed weather briefing, and once again everyone felt sure that mission would be scrubbed, for although the target area was clear, we were forecast to continue with zero conditions for takeoff and little improvement for landing nine hours later.

"Next, Group Operations gave us the formation lineup and the runway for takeoff. Then our group commander gave us some pertinent excerpts from the Combat Order and the composition of the task force, which contained 260 B-17s from groups of the 1st and 3rd Bombardment Divisions, with our group leading our wing, our division, and the 8th Air Force. He finished with a pep talk on flying a tight formation and making the most of our defenses. Lastly, he introduced Col. Budd Peaslee, who would fly with me as the 8th Air Force commander. Colonel Peaslee spoke briefly about the importance of destroying the target and about keeping our formation intact, then asked to speak to the lead and deputy lead crew alone.

"After the general briefing the navigators and bombardiers

went to their special detail briefing on the route and target areas. Colonel Peaslee met with my crew and the deputy lead crew, where he made it very clear that he was bent on destroying the target. His remarks were mostly made to the deputy lead crew, who would fly on our right wing. He gave them minute instructions on what to do if our lead plane was shot down. He tried to cover all possible contingencies, and we all left the meeting feeling that we had to get the job done. Our lead navigators and bombardiers then spent a few minutes studying the main target identification points to insure recognition when we arrived at the Initial Point.

"My regular copilot, Lieutenant Sperry, along with my gunners, had gone on out to our airplane to inspect it and to make certain that it was ready to go. Lieutenant Sperry was to act as tail gunner, chiefly to keep me informed as to what was happening to our formation and to let me know when someone was in trouble.

"I arrived at the airplane about thirty minutes before station time in order to make my own personal check of the ship and my crew. Technical Sergeant Edison was one of the most dependable men I met in the Army, and with his word I was immediately relieved of any doubt that all might not be right on board.

"I performed my normal walk-around inspection, then climbed in the rear hatch with my chute and flying equipment while noting that the weather had shown no improvement. In the meantime, Capt. Harry Hughes, navigator, and Lt. Edward T. O'Grady, bombardier, arrived from their last briefings.

"As we came aboard, we found the rest of our flight crew and the ground crew sitting inside, out of the rain, and one quick glance told me they were worried, scared, and that morale was down. I reassured them and told them that Colonel Peaslee was riding with us, to go sparingly on the oxygen so we'd have enough, cautioned them on interphone discipline, and then distributed the escape kits. Escape kits were issued to every combatant. Each kit contained German and French money, maps, water purifier, a compass, and a small pamphlet.

"The weather was so bad we all still doubted that we would go. Taxi time was rapidly approaching and Colonel Peaslee had not yet arrived, but I told Sergeant Edison to get into the copilot's seat and help me start the engines, since I knew we could not afford to be late. As we were starting the engines, the Colonel arrived and arranged his equipment while I allowed the engines to warm up and checked the instruments. We taxied out on the airfield. I pulled well up the runway to allow the others to fall in line behind in their takeoff positions. We still had about eight minutes before takeoff, which we used in checking the magnetos and electrical systems.

"I still couldn't believe we would attempt a takeoff, for the visibility was decreasing. Flight control had placed a red light at the far end of the runway to aid us in takeoff. At the last minute I broke radio silence to ask the tower if there was any message for us, hoping that we might be ordered to stand by. Frankly, I did not relish the idea of a zero-zero takeoff with a full bomb load, extra gasoline, and maybe bad icing conditions, realizing that with such weather conditions any of us would have trouble landing again in case of engine trouble or any kind of mechanical failure. Before the tower could answer, Harry reminded me that it was now takeoff time. I began to slowly rev my engines and, after a favorable answer from the tower, started down the runway.

"The next fifteen minutes were purely instrument flying. We climbed on course until we broke out on top at about seven thousand feet. We circled our low-frequency radio beacon, climbing to eighteen thousand feet, while the rest of our squadron airplanes joined our formation.

"As we climbed across the channel, we noticed high above us squadrons of Thunderbolts on their way to intercept any enemy aircraft that might come up to challenge us. While they were near, we rode along in comparative comfort, but about thirty minutes after we had crossed the enemy coast they reached their deepest point of penetration and had to leave us to go on alone. Then began what was later recorded as the greatest aerial battle of the war, for we were under constant attack from there to the target and halfway back to the coast, for about five hours.

"No sooner had the last P-47s left than six FW-190s appeared below and ahead of us. At first only one of these attacked, as the others were a bit slow in getting their altitude. Then they all began attacks, but they were not pressed home, and they failed to account for any of our formation.

"Presently two Me-210s appeared, escorted by twenty FW-190s and Me-190s. They began circling us, and my gunners were calling out attacks from all around the clock. Just then, well ahead to our left, we noticed the sky was filled with barrage-type flak. Colonel Peaslee asked Harry where it was coming from. He replied that it was the southern point of the Ruhr. At once we began a small right turn to make sure of avoiding it.

"Meantime, the right waist gunner, Staff Sergeant Ford, called out another enemy combat wing far behind us at five o'clock. By this time there were easily a hundred enemy aircraft attacking us, both twin-engine and single-engine! Reports of Forts going down were being called out on the interphone along with every type of fighter attack conceivable. I had noticed that the low group ahead of us had crossed the enemy coast with sixteen ships and had already lost five, with a sixth beginning to straggle. Just then Sergeant Ford yelled, 'Oh, Hell!' He reported that the enemy formation behind us were all twin-engine ships and that they were beginning to split up for a mass attack. That statement really stunned me for a moment, but we were being attacked so heavily by the enemy aircraft already there that I hardly had time to think about the future ones.

"Maj. George Ott, of South Dakota, our deputy leader, was flying on my right wing. Suddenly, while we were under an attack from the right by two 110s, an Me-109 came down out of the sun like a flash and knocked out one and possibly two of Major

Ott's engines. Immediately he began having trouble and could not keep up. He fell back and down. Nine chutes were counted to come from his ship as he went down under control. [That was the last time I saw him, until he attended a group reunion in Tampa, Florida. I told him he looked a lot better than the last time I had seen him.]

"Two Ju-88s came in at ten o'clock high. I called them out to Sergeant Edison in the top turret in time for him to send home some good shots that made them break off the attack. Harry yelled, 'My God, Mac, take some evasive action!' This I promptly did, as two rocket shells exploded off our nose.

"By this time we were getting our heaviest attacks. Almost every type of enemy fighter they had was there, including night fighters and fighter bombers. The low group ahead of us had now lost more than half of their ships, most of them exploding or burning in the air. Just then Staff Sergeant Van Horne in the ball turret said that Lieutenant Clough, leading the second element of our squadron, had been badly hit and was afire. Then he reported that an explosion in the left wing of Clough's ship had blown the wing off, and two chutes were reported coming from it. All the time we were being pounded by the German twin-engine fighters. These ships, attacking in groups of two to four and carrying two rocket guns each, were closing to about five hundred or six hundred yards from us and then letting go with a double salvo from each gun, leaving twin clouds of black smoke all around us. The single-engine fighters were making close frontal attacks, attempting to break up our formation, and finding plenty of 'easy meat' in the many stragglers left crippled by the rocket ships.

"We were still not more than halfway to the target, and with this situation at hand, we all realized that the chances for any of us to make it back to England were very slim. At one point Colonel Peaslee called me on the interphone and said, 'Captain, I think we've had it.'

"I didn't have much time to think about personal safety or about the safety of my crew. I had my hands full in trying to hold what was left of our formation together and maintain some kind of protective position behind the combat wing just ahead, as we had only two groups in our wing. But frankly I've never been more scared in all my life. In my glancing thoughts I looked at the situation: The ship on our right as well as the one under and behind us had been shot down. The low group ahead had only four ships left out of the sixteen they had crossed the coast with. The other groups had lost heavily. I couldn't see much hope for any of us if we had to go on under these conditions.

"Somehow we did manage to go on. I had pulled our formation up above and as close as possible behind the wing ahead, utilizing their protection against frontal attacks on us and in turn lending our protection against rear attacks on them. O'Grady called me about twenty minutes before the target to remind me to get the AFCE (Automatic Flight Control Equipment) set up at the first opportunity. I did this, but I had to unclutch it to take evasive action. The AFCE enabled the bombardier actually to control the airplane through the Norden bombsight during the bomb run into the target.

"Then Harry said that in about a minute we would start our bombing run. I clutched in the AFCE, made the turn toward the target, and told O'Grady that it was all his. By this time about half the enemy aircraft had left us, and those that were left had to replan their attack after we made our turn toward the target. I was busy holding a constant air speed and altitude and hoping we would do a good job. As we approached the target the flak began filling the sky ahead, but it was never very accurate. After I turned toward the target, Lieutenant O'Grady took over. This is his story of his bomb run:

"About ten minutes before the IP, Harry called me on the interphone, saying that the target wasn't very far off. It was quite apparent that the visibility was to be good, and I was glad. I guess I started to get a little excited. I had a mental picture of the target firmly in mind and started hoping for a good run. We made our turn into the target, and Mac called me and said, 'Okay O'Grady, it's all yours.' Harry, who in my opinion is one of the best naviga-tors in the world, called me and said, 'There it is, Ed—go get it.' For some reason I was looking at the wrong point, so I told him I didn't see it. He took his finger and pointed it out, and then sud-denly straight ahead was my mental picture, clear as a bell.

"I had my sight set up pretty well and the corrections were nil. The run I guess was what you'd call a bombardier's dream. Colonel Peaslee kept calling me saying, 'Get that target! Get it!' I checked in with Mac, asking the air speed, and then we were in our run. Fighters were everywhere, and twice on the run I could see enemy ships flying through my optics. The interphone was silent, but I could hear the gunners behind me firing away, and I felt pretty damn good about that.

"In the early part of our run the flak was light. Suddenly the flak started coming up, but I knew we had the target, and I felt great. I called 'Bombs away,' and our job had been done. The fighters kept coming in, and we were really catching hell. Enough has been said about the raid to know it was tough, and the way I like to describe it is that it's the first one I've ever made I knew I wasn't coming back from. I'll be a long time for-getting the most important minutes of my life, which happened between the time Mac, Captain MacLaughlin, said, 'You've got it,' and I answered, 'Bombs away.'

"When the small bomb signal light on the left of my panel flashed and O'Grady yelled, 'Bombs away,' I immediately began a right turn to get our formation together again before the fight-ers could begin attacking.

"We were hardly out of our turn before the fighters, mostly twin engine now, were hitting us. This time they failed to score and soon left us almost entirely to hit the groups behind us. Then for about ten minutes we went on with not a fighter in sight. We all knew that it wouldn't be long before they would be back, for now we were comparatively few in number, having lost nearly half our ships. So we waited and hoped that there wouldn't be too many of them.

"Then Lieutenant Sperry in the tail began calling them out from behind us. Some of them came around high and attacked from in front, coming down with great speed to avoid being hit themselves. Between attacks, Staff Sergeant Foley, the left waist gunner, asked Harry how long it would be before the P-47s would meet us. Harry hesitatingly replied, 'An hour and thirty-eight minutes.' I could almost feel the boys groan, although none made a sound. Little did we realize what might have happened had the Germans known our exact route back, for continued bad weather in England prevented the P-47 Thunderbolts from taking off to cover the last leg of our return flight.

"After we had gotten well into France on our return flight, the fighters broke off their attack, having accounted for three more of our bombers. From there on we had a sort of awed peace as we momentarily looked back, the view broken only by a few negligible bursts of flak against the white clouds below. The evening sun was bright in a clear blue sky, but we were not quite up to enjoying it.

"Finally we reached the Channel, although it was impossible to realize it by any visual means. That same front was still lying over England, and the Channel and all below was a solid mass of white clouds twelve thousand feet thick, mocking our every thought of landing. We were tired both physically and emotionally, and our oxygen supply was nearly gone. As we began our letdown some of the ships left our formation, for they were badly damaged or had injured men aboard who needed immediate attention. As we reached fifteen thousand feet, I took my mask and helmet off. We had been in the air for seven hours and on oxygen for more than six.

"O'Grady called the gunners to unload their guns and come out of their turrets as we crossed the English coast. They all came up front and opened a can of pineapple—the best pineapple the Dole Company ever canned!

"At last we found a hole in the clouds large enough to take the remainder of our formation down through. As we began our descent, we received a weather report from Headquarters, telling us that we could expect a ceiling of one thousand to two thousand feet and two miles visibility at our base. With this information we decided to let down below one thousand feet and go home.

"We let down over the south coast of England and started home. Gradually the visibility grew worse and the ceiling forced us below five hundred feet, with rain that made it very difficult to see. The formation stuck together, and even though we finally had to pull up into the clouds, the others pulled in close and stuck with me. I was almost ready to try to make it back to the south coast when Harry said he believed he could get us home by a series of radio fixes. After a number of small changes in course, he told me to start a gradual letdown on course. This I did, breaking out at six hundred feet within sight of our home field. We had practiced this once or twice in case we ever needed it. The others were able to follow me to within sight of the field. Then I instructed my rear element leader to land first, as he had an injured crewman and had lost an engine. I flew straight down the runway and circled at five hundred feet until all of my five aircraft landed, then came on in.

"No sooner had we touched the ground than Lieutenant O'Grady raised our flag from the astro-hatch. O'Grady's aunt had given him this American flag before his coming overseas. The flag had been blessed by his parish priest, we'd always flown with it, and we had come to consider it as our good luck charm. As the flag came up, Colonel Peaslee let out a cheer. You know how hearing the Star Spangled Banner can send chills up your spine; well, as we taxied around the perimeter of our airfield the various ground crews came to attention and smoothly saluted our flag. The scene gave me a strange thrill, and I felt that they were not only paying tribute to their flag but also to the men who had made the supreme sacrifice that day.

"As we taxied on to our dispersal area, Colonel Reid and Gen. Howard Turner, our combat wing C.O., met us, eagerly awaiting news of our trip and the missing ships. I shut off the engines and climbed out, trying to answer questions and shed flying clothing simultaneously.

"Technical Sergeant Germany, my crew chief, met me with his usual slow smile, which broadened as I marked up 'O.K. except for minor battle damage' on the Air Corps form 1A, which is the form for pilots' complaints against the mechanical condition of the ship. We had been very lucky, for our damage consisted of one twenty-millimeter hole in the tail, one small hole in the left wing, and one small hole in the side of the fuselage by my seat. Not one crew member had even a minor injury.

"My wing, the 40th Combat Wing, had left England with fifty-four aircraft, three groups of eighteen aircraft each. (Our low group, the 306th, had been unable to find us because of poor weather and visibility in the form-up area and had mistakenly joined another wing.) Upon landing, I had five aircraft left [out of eighteen] with three more landing at coastal bases due to injured airmen and or engines out. My other group, the 305th, landed with three aircraft and four more at other bases—from a total of eighteen at takeoff.

"Many important and highly destructive bombing missions were flown by the U.S. air forces in World War II, but this attack more than any other displayed the skill, courage, and leadership of American airmen, who—under continuous attack for nearly six hours—destroyed 70 percent of German ball bearing production while losing 25 percent of the bomber force.

"To me these men had character. They didn't dodge the draft, and when a tough mission came along they stood up to be counted. To me they were among the greatest Americans in history. They met their challenge.

"A few days later my squadron sent several crews to the 8th Air Force rest home for a week of rest and recuperation. The rest homes were operated by the American Red Cross and were a welcome change for us all. The officers' facility was known as

Stanbridge Earles and was located near Ramsey, Southampton. The land had been the site of the original home of King Ethelwulf, the father of Alfred the Great. The present home had been completely renovated by its prewar owner and appropriated by the British Air Ministry, who in turn made it available to the 8th Air Force. The manor house contained eighteen bedrooms and could accommodate up to thirty officers. Clean linens, luxurious baths, delicious food served on real silver and china made the place heaven compared to our normal lifestyle back at our air base. Our hostess was Pamela Humphrey Firman, of Cleveland, Ohio, a lovely lady of great charm and humor, who made all of us feel at home from the moment we arrived. Harry Hughes, Gus Ahrenholtz (a YB-40 pilot who had been assigned as my copilot), Eddie O'Grady, and I played golf and tennis during the days and bridge in the evenings. We had a really great week and returned to our base refreshed and rested and ready to bomb the Hun."

11

A New Base and My Longest Day

In early September we were alerted to move from our base at Alconbury. Our 325th Squadron had grown rapidly in numbers of radar-equipped Pathfinder airplanes and aircrews. They were now ready to become a group of their own, and we were to move on to our new base at Podington, about thirty miles west of Alconbury.

On September 15, 1943, our 92nd Bomb Group moved from Alconbury to Podington, leaving the Pathfinder group to become the 482nd Bomb Group. Col. Bascombe R. Lawrence, who had commanded our 92nd Group in May (while Colonel Reid was temporarily commander of 91st Group), became the new commander of the 482nd Pathfinder Group. Thus, in one year, our group had formed the 1/11th Combat Crew Replacement Center at Bovingdon, had moved and opened the base at Alconbury (where it tried and discarded the experimental YB-40), had established the new Radar Pathfinder Group, and now had moved on to Podington.

The airbase at Podington had been unused for some time, and it sure looked it. The living quarters were tar paper shacks, and most of the administrative buildings were Quonset huts. My operations building was the only modern building of any quality on the base.

The airfield had been built on the farms of the Orlebar family (on the west end) and of Lord Luke (on the east end). During this time, Lord Luke was away on duty with the British Army. Three generations of the Orlebars resided in their family manor, Hinwick House. They were very cordial, and I along with several other officers spent many happy hours there being hosted by their beautiful eighteen-year-old granddaughter, Eve Helps.

Forty years later, I joined Lord Luke as a speaker at a memorial dedication ceremony. He too was most cordial. Margaret Thatcher was running for her last term as prime minister, and the London papers were giving her a very rough time. I told Lord Luke how much I admired her and that I thought I'd send her a small check for her campaign. His eyes brightened and he said, "That would indeed be a grand gesture, she would so very much appreciate it, and it would be a really lovely thing to do." Then his eyes narrowed, and he said, "If you do send her a contribution, please mention my name." I did send her a check, and I mentioned Luke's name and sent him a copy of my letter.

Podington was to be our base for the remainder of the war, and we all went about making it as comfortable as possible.

Sometime during the last week in October, Col. William "Darky" Reid called me to his office and told me he was reassigning me to the Group Headquarters Squadron as assistant group operations officer. I was elated to be selected for this new position, but it meant I'd be leaving all of my old combat mates and would again be working for Lt. Col. Bob Keck, the officer who had almost bailed out and left us en route home from our first raid on Lille, France, a year earlier.

Maj. Wilson Todd, of Richmond, Virginia, had been the assistant group operations officer but had become commander of the 327th Squadron. Ten days later, on November 5, he was shot down while leading the group to attack a target at Gelsenkirchen.

He luckily was able to bail out and spent a year and a half as a prisoner of war.

As assistant group operations officer, in addition to helping plan and brief the raids our group participated in, I was also now designated an air commander and placed in the rotation cycle of leaders for the future raids.

On November 16, we briefed a raid to Norway, to attack the molybdenum mines at Knaben. The entire 8th Air Force Bomber Command was attacking Norway that day. While our 1st Bomb Division was attacking Knaben, the 2nd Bomb Division's B-24s were attacking airfields near Oslo, and the 3rd Bomb Division's B-17s were attacking the heavy water atomic plant at Rjuken. (Heavy water was crucial to the extraction of fissionable material from uranium.)

Our group was scheduled to lead our 40th Combat Wing, and Maj. McGehee Word was selected to fly as air commander with the 326th Squadron, leading our group. I was selected as the deputy air commander and assigned to fly with Lt. William B. Lock and crew on the leader's right wing. It appeared to be an easy flight for all of us, for our route was well out over the North Sea, away from German defenses, and Intelligence told us that there were very few fighter airplanes and flak guns in our target area.

Our takeoff and formation join-up were normal. We climbed to our assigned altitude of eighteen thousand feet and began our flight northeast up the center of the North Sea as briefed. It was a beautiful, bright, and sunny November day. We could see for miles, but the hundreds of icebergs dotting the sea in all directions left a rather somber aura among the aircrews—for we knew all too well that no human could survive in those icy waters if we had to bail out or ditch the airplane in the sea. As we flew farther north we began to encounter cumulus clouds below us. They were no problem en route but worried us since they might hide our target. Little did I realize what a godsend they'd be to me on the way home an hour later.

As we neared the Norwegian shore, the clouds disappeared,

and so did everything else that might have been discernible. All of Norway was covered with thick blankets of new snow glistening in the bright sunshine like a huge white diamond. Not a road, railroad, building, or town was recognizable. Even the lakes were so well covered they couldn't be seen. As our formation began to descend to our briefed bombing altitude of fifteen thousand feet, Major Word radioed me that they were having trouble locating the Initial Point, from which to begin the bomb run, and also that they could not see the target. The navigator on Lieutenant Lock's crew could not see it either. We circled the entire formation while everyone searched for the target.

Suddenly, the flight engineer on our airplane noted the oil pressure on our number three engine was falling at a rapid rate. We elected to shut it down and feather the propeller (feathering turned the leading edge of the prop blades to the wind) so that it wouldn't turn and thus would provide the least resistance to further flight. As we reduced power and shut off fuel to that engine, I pushed the feathering button. To our horror the propeller did not feather, and repeated attempts to feather it were futile. There were no fighters around and no flak guns shooting at us, so I radioed Major Word of our problem and told him we would have to drop out of formation because, with a windmilling propeller and a loaded airplane, we could not adequately keep formation. He called back and said they had just located the target and to try to keep formation so that we could get all of our bombs on the target.

Flying Officer Tim Eaton, the navigator on Major Word's lead airplane, located the target when the powerhouse at the mines had to release steam. The steam itself was not discernible, but it cast a shadow, and Eaton quickly figured out what it was. He was our group's top navigator. Lieutenant Lock then had to use 90 percent power on the other three engines to hold formation position until the bomb drop. By the time we dropped our bombs, the propeller on our number three engine had been windmilling for perhaps ten minutes without any lubrication, because the engine was inoperable and no oil was being pumped to the whirling propeller. The dead engine had begun to heat up from the friction of the windmilling propeller, and the entire engine case was turning a dull red color.

I knew that we could not continue to run our three engines at such extremely high power settings. With the formation preparing to climb back to eighteen thousand feet, and no German fighters in sight, I elected to pull out of the formation so we could reduce our engine speeds to a normal cruise level. I called Major Word and told him of my plan to proceed home alone and that I'd meet him there.

I then asked the navigator for a heading straight west to Scotland so that we'd have the minimum time over the North Sea. He quickly gave me 270 degrees, which I thought couldn't be correct at that latitude. Before I could discuss the new heading I noticed some small puffs of smoke erupting about one hundred feet to our right, and I called the gunners in rear of the airplane and asked who was shooting at us. They answered, "Oh, sir, there's an M-E [Messerschmitt] behind us shooting at us." I immediately asked why they weren't returning the fire, and they replied, "Sir, we threw all the guns overboard to make the airplane lighter." For an instant my heart sank, for I felt sure this guy would get us. By this time we were crossing the coast westbound, with hundreds of icebergs in view. There were a few rounds of inaccurate flak being fired at us—just enough to keep the fighter at a distance. We were over a coastal city, and I could see an airport nearby. Lieutenant Lock called me on the interphone and said, "Sir, let's go down and land before we either get shot down in this icy water or this engine catches fire and we have to bail out into the North Sea." I said, "I only have one more mission to finish my tour, and I want to go home." The lone fighter that had dropped back to avoid the flak followed us for a short distance but never got close enough to damage us, because he didn't want to take any chances on our shooting him down around those icebergs either.

Once out over the sea, I began to concentrate on our sick engine, which by now was white with heat. I instructed Lieutenant Lock to slow the airplane down to 105 miles per hour to try to lessen the propeller revolutions per minute and the engine heat. I also told him to stay just above the present clouds, so that if any fighters showed up we could fly into those icy clouds. I told him to be sure to stay just out of the clouds, because I knew our windows would immediately freeze over if we got into them, as the temperature was about thirty-five degrees below zero at our altitude.

Shortly, the engine became so hot that the propeller froze and stopped turning. The engine immediately began to cool, and for a few minutes I thought maybe we had at last solved our problem. I then returned to check the heading we were on and found nearly fifty degrees of magnetic declination on our course and soon turned our airplane to a new heading for Scotland. A moment later we struck a convection current near the cloud tops. The propeller freed itself and began to windmill again, and of course the engine started becoming white hot again. I began to become truly alarmed, for I knew we were at least two hours from Scotland, and I knew there was a great chance that the oil or hydraulic lines would catch fire. I said a few silent prayers while pretending not to be concerned, to keep the crew from panicking.

While I was discussing our engine problem with the engineer, Lieutenant Lock suddenly flew us into the top of a cloud. I instinctively looked at our flight instruments, and they had all spilled and were not working. Lieutenant Lock had failed to switch the vacuum system from the dead engine to the number two engine. He immediately turned the vacuum lever to the number two engine, and the instruments soon repositioned themselves. We wallowed through the cloud and, by opening our side windows, found our way out again, but it took another ten minutes before the ice wore off our windshields so we could see straight ahead.

At this point I was really shaken. Suddenly one of the crew called out, "Fighters below us!" As I scanned the dark waters I caught a glimpse of two twin engine Me-110s, flying parallel patterns along our same course at what I estimated to be maybe one thousand feet above sea level. The German radar along the coast was probably spotting us and directing the fighters, but radar in those days could not read altitude. The fighters expected us to descend to low altitudes to evade the radar, and they hoped to catch us there. Instead, we were sitting above those big, broken cumulus clouds, where they could not see us. We had done one thing right that day!

Our one dead propeller kept windmilling and freezing to a stop, then cooling would contract the metal and the propeller would start up again. The engine case would go from a dull red to a bright red and on to white and then repeat the same cycle again. I was numb from tension and fear and the super-cold temperature at that altitude. I felt sure our time had come, and I thought of my family and loved ones that I'd never see again. Finally, the western horizon began to grow dark, and the navigator told me we were about sixty miles from Scotland. Though the sky ahead looked threatening, with perhaps storms over the northeast mountains of Scotland, I figured our best chance was to get over the Scottish mountains and bail out if our engine caught fire. As we drew nearer I realized that our chance of survival in the deep snow of those mountains was also minimal.

At that time I instructed Lieutenant Lock to fly on a southerly course, as close as he could to the coast while staying out of the icy clouds, and if our engine caught fire we'd fly inland and bail out. Presently the weather began to improve, and we were soon overland with good visibility, still flying at only 100 to 110 miles per hour, nursing our overheated engine. Our navigator quickly located our position and gave us a direct course to our base, still a hundred miles away. We had called a "Mayday" and told them of our plight, and they gave us a steer to the nearest airbase. I had already told Lieutenant Lock that we'd land at the first airfield we could find, and I had instructed the crew to be on the lookout for any airfield.

J. Kemp McLaughlin, Cmdr. Air National Guard of West
Virginia, 1947–1977. (U.S. Air National Guard photo)

(Top) J. Kemp McLaughlin at graduation from flight school, Columbus Army Airfield, Miss., 1942. (Right) Damaged B-17 after mid-air collision with plane piloted by Lt. Gene Wiley, October 9, 1942. Pilot James Dempsey of Wilson, N.C. stands at left. Lt. James B. Foster of New Castle, Penn., stands at right.(U.S. Army Air Corps photos)

Aircrews of the 407th Squadron at the October 9, 1942, briefing for the raid on Lille, France. This was to be their first combat mission. (U.S. Army Air Corps photo)

Crew, passengers, and hosts following our B-17 crash in Ireland (top). Kemp McLaughlin is kneeling in front. Note the wrecked stone fence behind the left wing. (U.S. Army Air Corps photo)

Col. William Reid, Capt. Kemp McLaughlin, and Maj. Edward "Bushface" Jones, group navigator, await the return of a raid from atop the control tower, 1943. (U.S. Army Air Corps photo)

McLaughlin's crew in 1943: *Front, left to right,* S/Sgt. Brubaker, Ford Vanhorn, and Foley. *Back, left to right,* T/Sgt. Eidson, Lt. Ed. T. O'Grady, Capt. Kemp McLaughlin, and Capt. Henry Hughes. Missing, co-pilot Augustus Ahrenholz. (U.S. Army Air Corps photo)

En route to a target in Germany, 1943. Target unknown. (U.S. Army Air Corps photo)

B-17s climbing across the English Channel. Note the German coast at the top of picture. (U.S. Army Air Corps photo)

B-17s on the bomb run. The airplanes had to hold a steady heading from the Initial Point to the target while continually being shot at. (U.S. Army Air Corps photo)

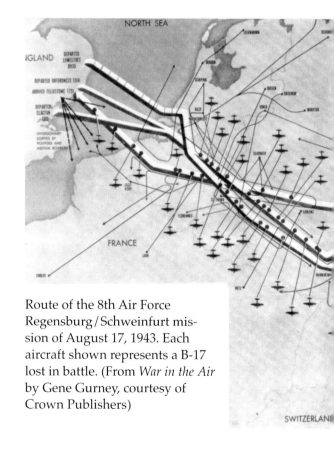

Route of the 8th Air Force Regensburg/Schweinfurt mission of August 17, 1943. Each aircraft shown represents a B-17 lost in battle. (From *War in the Air* by Gene Gurney, courtesy of Crown Publishers)

(Top) The lead squadron dropping its bombs, as seen from the low squadron. Heavy contrails trail behind from our exhaust heat. (U.S. Army Air Corps photo)

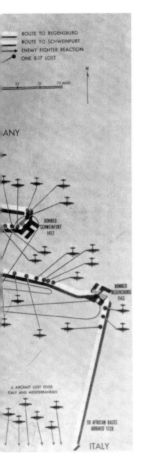

Bombs away at the end of the bomb run. (U.S. Army Air Corps photo)

Target, Gdynia, Poland, October 9, 1943. Note all the ships leaving the docks before the bombs hit. (U.S. Army Air Corps photo)

Bombs on target. Laon/Athies Airfield, France. (U.S. Army Air Corps photo)

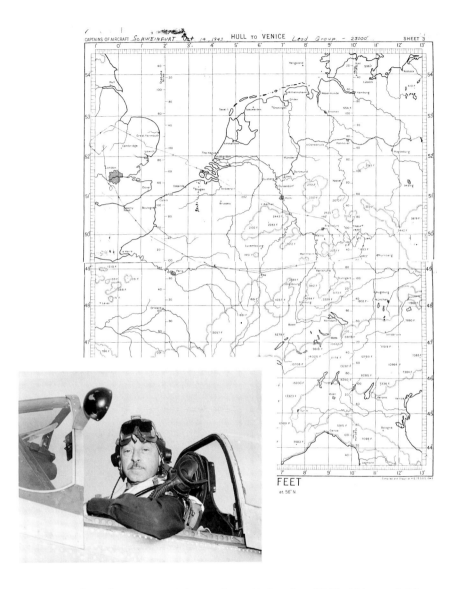

(Above, right) The route to Schweinfurt, 14 October 1943. (Above, left) Col. Budd Peaslee, deputy commander of the 40th Combat Wing, 1st Air Division, who flew with me to Schweinfurt, Germany, on 14 October 1943 as air commander. He later flew deep into Germany in this P-51 Mustang with only a lone wingman to report the weather to the following bombers. (U.S. Army Air Corps photos)

Stanbridge Earles, the American Red Cross Aircrew Rest Home in Ramsey, England. (U.S. Army Air Corps photo)

Pamela Humphrey Firman, hostess at Stanbridge Earles. (U.S. Army Air Corps photo)

Dinner at Stanbridge Earles, the Aircrew Rest Home. Dining with real linen, silver, and crystal was a far cry from our 92nd officers mess. (U.S. Army Air Corps photo)

Left to right, Gus Ahrenholz, copilot; Kemp McLaughlin; Pam Firman, hostess; Edward T. O'Grady, bombardier; and Henry A. Hughes, navigator. This picture was taken the week after the October 14, 1943, raid on Schweinfurt. It was a much needed rest. (U.S. Army Air Corps photo)

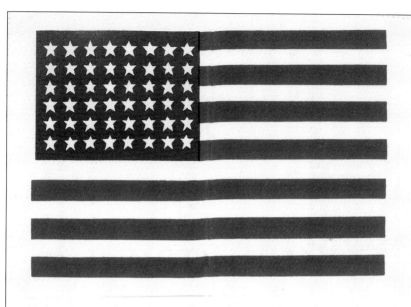

Я американец

" Ya Amerikánets " *(Pronounced as spelt)*

Пожалуйста сообщите сведения обо мне в Американскую Военную Миссию в Москве

Please communicate my particulars to American Military Mission Moscow

Aircrew indentification tag for crews on shuttle flights to Russia, 1943–1944. (Author's collection)

Leaflet dropped in Germany telling the Germans of our
bombing power and asking them to give up the war.
(Author's collection)

Little friends—P-47 escorts en route to target. (U.S. Army Air Corps photo)

Flack to the right of us, flack to the left of us, but on charged the B-17s to Merseburg in 1944. (U.S. Army Air Corps photo)

Bombs away over Germany, 1944. Target unknown. (U.S. Army Air Corps photo)

Beginning descent for home base after a raid. Group formations usually descended in flights of three airplanes when under instrument conditions. (U.S. Army Air Corps photo)

A Pathfinder B-17 from the 92nd Bomb Group with a H2X radar antenna on the bottom of the airplane. (U.S. Army Air Corps photo)

Radar bombing from above the undercast. Poor weather often required radar bombing, but the technique of the day was far from precision bombing. (U.S. Army Air Corps photo)

(Above) Capt. John Bosko's B-17 was damaged by flak at Merseburg, Germany, in August 1944. Captain Bosko had a long career as an airline pilot after the war. (Right) *Left,* Capt. Charles Beynon, group navigator. *Right,* Maj. Julian Thornton, group bombardier. (U.S. Army Air Corps photos)

Painting on the wall of 326th Squadron Operations at Podington Aerodrome. It was moved to the American Air Museum at Duxford, England, in 1996. (U.S. Army Air Corps photo)

Date 5th October 1944

TARGET INFORMATION SHEET

G E R M A N Y

Op. No. GN 3770	Place BERCHTESGADEN Nr. SALZBURG	Lat. : 47° 37' N
A.M. No. 3(k)20	Category LAND ARMAMENTS	Long. : 13° 02' E
D.T.M. No. -	Sub-catgy. Military Establishments	Alt. : 6,050 ft. Target A 3,200 ft. Target B

ALL PREVIOUS INFORMATION SHEETS AND AMENDMENTS THERETO ARE CANCELLED.

TARGET MAP	STANDARD 1941 (MAGNETIC) TYPE MAP DATED JULY 1944.
DESCRIPTION	(i) The TARGET comprises a complex of two individual targets as follows:-

A. The EAGLES NEST on the OBER KEHL ALP

B. WACHENFELS at the village of OBER SALZBURG.

Target A is 2 miles S.E. of BERCHTESGADEN, 13 miles S. of SALZBURG

Target B is 2 miles E. of BERCHTESGADEN, and 12 miles S. of SALZBURG. Both targets are situated in a remote part of the mountainous country lying to the S. of Salzburg. Target A is situated on the extreme top of the Ober Kehl Alp, which is a spur 6,000 ft. high running N.W. from 8,300 ft. high Hoher Goll, which forms the frontier between Germany and Austria. Further S. still, beyond the 6 mile long lake of the Königs-See, is the 8,800 ft. range of the Steinernes Meer.

Neither target is adjacent to any built up area, but to the E. of Target B are several hutted camps.

(ii)   Target A, sometimes also known as the "Tea-House", was built by Hitler as an observation post and place of entertainment for guests. It is stated to be inaccessible from the outside, and a considerable part of the building is believed to be buried in the top of the mountain. The approach to the Eagle's Nest is by way of a road (not shown on the G.S.G.S.100,000 scale map) which leads to a point on the mountain side from which a tunnel is driven in to the mountain to a point immediately below the Eagle's Nest itself. From this point a lift rises some 400 ft. to the Eagle's Nest. The building contains kitchens, sitting-rooms etc., but before the war was not normally used as a place of residence. Outside the building, which has six large windows, is a broad covered stone balcony, from which views of the Hoher Göll and the Königs See can be obtained.

Target B is an area containing the Führer's residence, Wachenfels. The area is approached by a winding road from Berchtesgaden and includes extensive barracks and other buildings for guards and servants. The actual Haus Wachenfels is the building marked 1 on illus. 3(k)20/4.

(iii)   Target A (See illus. 3(k)20/2) is an extremely small objective apparently measuring about 17 yds. square.

Target B (See illus. 3(k)20/4) is about 915 x 415 yds. with the major axis in an E.N.E. direction. It contains 6 principal groups of buildings of which Nos. 1-3 are residential and No. 1 is the Führer's residence. Nos. 4-6 are respectively a hospital, a garage and a group of S.S. barracks. The area is evidently closely guarded, and some parts of it are surrounded by a substantial wall.

Information is not at present available regarding detailed particulars of Obstructions to low flying attacks in the area of this target complex, and rather than delay the issue of this Information Sheet, this data is being omitted for the present. If this information is required for this particular target, it will be obtained and supplied at short notice on application to A.I.3c(1)

/Attention

A.I.3.c. (1)

Order to bomb the Eagle's Nest and Wachenfels, near Berchtesgaden, 1944. This raid was never flown. (U.S. Army Air Corps photo)

Lt. Horace Spencer and crew with General Patton after being shot down. (U.S. Army Air Corps photo)

إلى كل عربي كريم

السلام عليكم ورحمة الله وبعد فحامل هذا الكتاب من جيش الولايات المتحدة وهو صديق لكل الشعوب العربية فنرجوأن تحسنوا معاملته وتحافظوا عليه من كل الأضرار وأن تقدموا له الطعام والشراب وترشدوه إلى أقرب معسكر أمريكي أو بريطاني وستكافئكم بسخاء على خدماتكم والسلام عليكم ورحمة الله وبركاته.

FRANKLIN D. ROOSEVELT
رئيس الولايات المتحدة الأمريكية

To all Arab peoples greetings and peace be upon you. The bearer of this letter is a soldier of the United States Government and a friend of all Arabs. Treat him well, guard him from harm, give him food and drink, help him to return to the nearest American or British soldiers and you will be liberally rewarded. Peace and the mercy of God be upon you.
FRANKLIN D. ROOSEVELT,
President of the United States of America.

Salut a tous les Arabes, que la paix soit avec vous. Le porteur de cette lettre est un soldat du Gouvernement des Etats Unis et un ami de tous les Arabes. Traitez le bien et protégez le, donnez lui à boire et à manger, aidez le à retourner au poste Americain ou Anglais le plus proche et vous serez génereusement recompensé. Que la paix et la bénédiction de Dieu soit avec vous.
FRANKLIN D. ROOSEVELT,
Président des Etats Unis.

Leaflet used in the North African invasion asking the North Africans for help. (U.S. Army Air Corps photo)

Maj. Julian Thornton, group bombardier, 1943–1944. (U.S. Army Air Corps photo)

Maj. Raphael "Cold Front" Kernan, group meteorologist. Kernan had a long career with the U.S. Weather Service after the war. (U.S. Army Air Corps photo)

Lt. Col. Albert Cox, Cmdr. 325th Squadron, 1944–1945, now retired in North Carolina. (U.S. Army Air Corps photo)

Lt. Col. James Smyrl, Cmdr. 327th Bomb Squadron, 1944–1945. (U.S. Army Air Corps photo)

Maj. Don Parker, Cmdr. 407th Bomb Squadron, 1943–1944. Don played halfback for Ball State University before the war. After the war he ran his own automobile parts company. (U.S. Army Air Corps photo)

Col. James Sutton, Cmdr. 92nd Bomb Group, 1942–1943. (U.S. Army Air Corps photo)

Col. William M. Reid, Comdr.
92nd Bomb Group, 1943–1944.
(U.S. Army Air Corps photo)

Col. James W. Wilson, Cmdr.
92nd Bomb Group, 1944–1945.
(U.S. Army Air Corps photo)

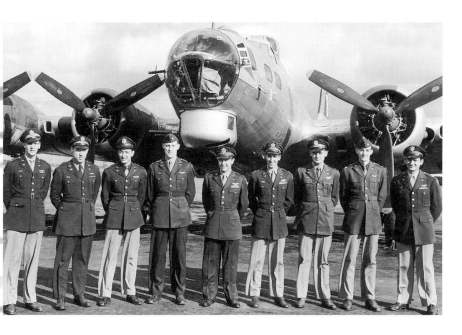

Commanders and staff, 92nd Bomb Group, October 1944. *Left to right,*
Maj. Charles Beynon, group navigator; Lt. Col. E.C. Hardin, Cmdr. 326th
Squadron; Lt. Col. William Nelson, Cmdr. 407th Squadron; Maj. Kemp
McLaughlin; Col. James W. Wilson, Cmdr.; Lt. Col. Rip Riordan, Deputy
Cmdr.; Lt. Col. Jim Smyrl, Cmdr. 327th Squadron; Lt. Col. Al Cox, Cmdr.
325th Squadron; Lt. Col. Julian Thornton, group bombardier. (U.S. Army
Air Corps photo)

Group Commader Col. James
W. Wilson congratulates the
Major McLaughlin upon
completion of his last mis-
sion, February 1945. (U.S.
Army Air Corps photo)

B-17 group in formation flight. (U.S. Army Air Corps photo)

Our spirits had risen immeasurably by this time, and we were descending to two thousand feet when we spotted an airfield up ahead. We quickly called the tower and asked for landing instructions and any fire-fighting equipment available. As we approached the landing end of the runway and lifted the nose of the ship to the landing attitude, and as the airspeed slowed to about eighty miles per hour, the hot engine burst into flames. The relief that came over me as the wheels touched the ground made me feel like crying for joy, even though the engine not ten feet from me was burning furiously. When we came to a stop, the fire truck began squirting fire-repellent foam on the engine, cutting off the oxygen and bringing it under control. Lieutenant Lock asked me if he shouldn't taxi off the runway, and I said, "Lord no, let her burn to the ground right here. I never want to see this airplane again." Once we were out of the plane, the fire crew soon had the fire out and were preparing to tow the airplane to the ramp as some British lorries came to pick us up. The airfield we had landed on had no operating units at that time and thus very little activity or equipment.

We soon got to the control tower and called our base at Podington, and in a short while we had an airplane en route to get us. It was now nearly 4 P.M., and we'd been in the air with an engine ready to explode at any minute since noon. I was so wrung out from the experience that I could hardly move. I desperately wanted to go lie down and be alone with peace and quiet for awhile. Of all the raids I had flown, and with all the close calls I'd had, this one was the toughest. It was indeed my longest day.

Sadly, William B. Lock and his crew were shot down while returning from a raid on Oschersleben on January 11, 1944. Only five parachutes were seen leaving his burning airplane.

12

Group Operations

Group Operations was the heart of the entire bomb group organization. Every unit on the base operated in support of our planes and schedules. Our Group Operations facility consisted of offices for the group navigators, group bombardiers, a large planning room, and of course a briefing room large enough to accommodate twenty-five crews of ten men each. In addition we were supported by Group Intelligence, Weather, Communications, Engineering, and Ordinance.

Typically we'd receive an alert notice in the late afternoon. Next, if we were lucky, we'd receive instruction on the type and quantity of bombs to put on the airplanes in order for Ordinance to get on with the job. Loading twenty-one airplanes with sixty-six hundred pounds of bombs each takes a while. Every now and then Bomber Command would decide to change the bomb load, usually at about one o'clock in the morning, and the poor Ordinance people would have to unload the airplanes and then reload them again. I yearned for the night that some of the headquarters officers might have to help do such a job. Then about ten o'clock that evening we'd get the combat order giving us the target, the route, the participating units, other units' targets, fighter escort cover, times, coordinates of en route points, and communications instruction.

The Bomber Command order would normally give us a departure time for Control Point 1, which usually was the point on the English coast over which we would fly outbound. Our division and wing would then plan our takeoff routes and formation form-up points and altitudes, with departure times for each so that we could form a group. We would then fly to another point to join our wing, then on to the third point to join our division, and all depart Control Point 1 close enough together to protect each other and to enable our escort fighters to properly cover us. On paper it seemed to be such an easy plan, but in practice it was very difficult to execute because there were so many variables such as weather interference, mechanical failures, unexpected wind shifts, and radio failures.

After receiving the field order from Bomber Command, I would call each squadron operations officer and ask for a list of crew and airplanes from each for that raid. Each would then bring me his respective squadron formation plan, showing who would lead and in which position each crew would fly. In the meantime, Intelligence would prepare the map board display, showing the route to be used and enemy defenses. During the night, the group navigator would prepare the exact route to our form-up area, and on to wing join-up, and then to Control Point 1, with times and altitudes to be flown. The aircrews would be awakened about three hours prior to takeoff. They would then be taken to breakfast and on to mission briefing two hours before takeoff.

I would usually open the briefing by announcing the target bomb load and generally describing the takeoff and form-up plan and communications data with codeword call signs and recall codes. The call sign for our group was Bull Pen Blue. The 305th and the 306th Groups of the 40th Combat Wing were Bull Pen Red and Bull Pen White. At the end of the briefing our group commander and the officer flying as air commander for the raid would usually speak, emphasizing tight formation for better protection and close formation on the bomb run from the Initial Point to the target, to provide a good bomb pattern.

Intelligence would give numbers of flak guns and fighters in each area and point out areas to stay away from. They would also brief on escape and evasion, give out escape kits in case one had to bail out, and point out the best routes to neutral countries such as Sweden and Switzerland. Each of these countries had received many bombers and crews by the time the war ended.

At the close of the general briefing, the group navigator would give a time hack (countdown) so that every one could set his watch and all would be operating on the same time. Then the group navigator and the group bombardier would provide a specialized briefing for their respective charges on target identification, approach to the Initial Point, and bomb run. Identifying small targets through the haze, smoke, and sometimes broken clouds from five miles up is very difficult. It was of great importance that the lead navigator and bombardier be on track as they arrived at the Initial Point so that the bombardier have time not only to see his target, but also to kill the wind drift. This procedure would allow the entire formation to fly a straight line into the target so that the bombs, when released, would fall straight toward the target and not drift left or right.

Each crewman then drew his parachute, Mae West, and flak jacket, knelt for the chaplain's prayer, and was trucked to his airplane. I usually went to the control tower to observe the takeoff and handle any last-minute changes along with my group commander and his assistant.

After takeoff, it was my duty to meet any airplanes to see why they returned and to determine what penalties if any were to be given to the crews that returned early for insufficient reasons. Early returnees were always a minor problem. Fear was the reason for most of them, and the smallest mechanical failure, such as high cylinder-head temperatures or oil overflow from high temperatures on takeoff or climb-out, would bring a nervous pilot home early nearly every time. These early returnees were called abortions. The pilot of one early returnee that I recall gave me the excuse that he was temporarily blinded. He told me that out over the Channel he was unable to see the other airplanes in his formation. I asked him how he managed to land his airplane, and he explained that when he got back down to sea level he had regained his eyesight! I assessed him three extra missions, but later I told his squadron commander to remove the penalty. Only by holding each pilot personally responsible could we control the abortion fever.

After dealing with early returnees I would go to my quarters and try to get some much-needed sleep before the airplanes returned from their mission. This became a routine that would eventually wear on me mentally and physically, especially as the frequency of missions increased and I found myself working all night nearly every night, with only a little sleep in the daytime.

December 1943 arrived, and I celebrated my twenty-fifth birthday on the seventh. We had been at war nearly two years, and we were beginning to land some solid blows in our air war against Germany, but at a terrible price. I had lucked out through twenty-four missions and had only one more to go to finish my tour. I also got quite a surprise when I received a promotion to Major in late November. I had written my folks and sweetheart that I'd soon be home, when Colonel Reid informed me that he would not let me fly my last mission because he needed me to stay there and help run group operations. My morale dropped a few degrees that day.

Pam Humphrey invited me to Stanbridge Earles for Christmas. It was only for three days but most enjoyable. No combat crews were scheduled there at Christmas, so the rest home staff invited in a few friends, and we had a wonderful Christmas house party.

13

Escape and Evasion

When Col. William M. Reid was transferred from the 91st Group back to the 92nd Group, Lt. Col. Dave Alford was sent to the 91st Group as its group operations officer. Here is his story of his escape and evasion after being shot down:

"The mission at the time was to bomb railroad yards at Frankfurt, Germany. I was the operations officer of the 91st Bomb Group, at Bassingbourne, part of the 1st Wing of the 1st Division, 8th Air Force. Since the 91st Bomb Group was scheduled to lead the wing on this particular mission, I was scheduled to be wing leader, along with the group navigator, Capt. Dave Williams. In this particular instance, we had some B-17s equipped with the H2X bomb device, which we commonly called the Pathfinder. These planes were all assigned to one particular group, the 482nd Bomb Group, and when we were scheduled to be wing lead, they would send one airplane over to us. We would put our leader and navigator in, and the rest of the crew would belong to the 482nd.

"Lieutenant Bock [now living in Houston, Texas] was the pilot of the particular Pathfinder airplane that day. I flew as copilot. Captain Williams and I got aboard, and we proceeded on our way. There were no difficulties until we got over enemy territory, where we began to experience some fighter opposition and quite a bit of flak, which was normal. Our route was north of the Ruhr Valley and on down into Frankfurt. Over the target, we did receive considerably more flak and a bit more fighter opposition. But we flew on, and after we got to the target area we could see visually and proceeded to drop our bombs—all except four or five airplanes, which did not release for one reason or another not known to me (probably some malfunction in the bomb-release devices). Consequently, we went over the target, turned around, and started back toward England, a course to the northwest.

"We had had problems with the radar equipment all the way across, trying to navigate over an undercast, and at the time we dropped our bombs it almost went out completely. However, we did proceed back toward England, picked a target of opportunity, and dropped the rest of the bombs, then continued on course. Unfortunately, with the equipment malfunctioning so much, we encountered a very strong northwest wind that blew us off course. So we continued to get hit strongly when we got over the Ruhr Valley, in the area of Cologne, and finally our airplane got shot up so badly we had to leave the formation.

"After we were hit, we had a fire in the nose and a fire in the right wing. We decided to leave the formation. We put the wheels down and entered the clouds around twenty-five thousand feet. About this time, the pilot was hit and went into a state of shock, or so it seemed, and shortly thereafter he passed out completely. I was not quite sure what was wrong. I thought perhaps he might be dead, but after we got down a way he came to, and we determined that his oxygen line had been severed with some flak that came through into the cockpit, and at that point he seemed very rational.

"Incidentally, flying in that same formation that day was my cousin, Frank Alford, who had come to the theater about a year and a half after I did. Since I knew some people he was assigned to in another group, I managed to get him assigned to my group, the 91st. I believe this was the second mission he had flown with us, and he was flying just above me. On the first mission that Frank flew, they got shot up pretty badly—the crew and the airplane—and they barely landed on the English coast way down from us. I was thinking at that point that I would need to write my uncle and aunt (his parents) and tell them what happened. Since they did get back, and everything went fine, it turned out that as I was going down, there was Frank, sitting up there above me in high flight, and it was going to be *his* job to write *my* parents and tell them what had happened! So things have a way of turning themselves around a little bit. Fortunately, Frank finished all of his missions and came home safely.

"About this time, it was quite evident that we needed to bail out, and I so ordered the crew, which they did, not knowing where we were, but figuring we were still over Germany someplace, because we hadn't been very far from target when all this antiaircraft fire hit us. I asked Dave Williams to help the pilot get out, which he did. Dave was the last one to jump. He asked me if I was going and I said, 'Of course, as soon as you get out!' Well, Dave jumped, and then I left the copilot's seat, where I'd been all the time, and started back to bail out through the bomb bay. About halfway back, I looked around, and my parachute was strewn out between the seats and in the aisle, and there was no way in the world that I could bail out with that kind of a situation. Consequently, I crawled back into the pilot's seat, and sat down in a pool of blood left there by Lieutenant Bock, and I decided I had to fly the airplane down.

"To say that I flew the airplane down is not quite right. It glided down, because two engines were out, and I never did put the power on to the other two engines. If I had known then what I discovered later, I probably could have flown that airplane back to England with two engines, provided I didn't get shot down by a bunch of fighters someplace, because the fire in the wing, which looked about the size of a number two washtub, apparently was a severed fuel line. The fuel had been set afire by the supercharger, and it was really burning more fuel than it was burning the airplane itself. As most people would anticipate, and as most of us had seen in this situation, other airplanes had exploded in the air, so I figured the best way to salvation was to get that thing on the ground as quickly as possible. I proceeded to do this, and went down through the clouds and broke out somewhere between five hundred and one thousand feet. I was mostly over woods, and I saw some houses and a few villages. My windshield had iced over completely in the front, but the windows on either side were clear. I spotted an open field out the right window, made a right turn, and bounced the airplane into the field, which turned out to be a dairy farm.

"I finally came to rest without turning it over or anything else. This was a great bit of luck. The time of my landing was sometime around 1:30 in the afternoon, and when the plane stopped I jumped from the window down to the ground and ran from the airplane, thinking it would explode any moment. As I ran I threw away my helmet and goggles into a little pond, because I immediately knew they would be telltale evidence of who I was and that surely the Germans would be looking for this airplane very shortly, because smoke was beginning to go pretty high up into the air. People had begun to gather already when I came to a halt, so I ran and warned them to stay out of the way the best way I could, that it might blow up. Then I got to the edge of the woods and jumped a fence.

"I didn't really know where I was going, but I jumped the fence, and unfortunately I landed in about two tons of cow manure. I was in Holland, in dairy country, and they accumulate their cow manure on the dairy farms in great big piles, and that's what they use for the most part for their fertilizer. Then, in the winter (it was February 4) the leaves had accumulated on top of it so it was not recognizable. Consequently, I ended up over my ankles, almost up to my knees, in cow manure, which was kept soft, naturally, by the constant rain, snow, and sleet. Trying to get out, I fell forward, and went in up to my elbows. I finally struggled free of this muck and started down a dirt road, not knowing where I was going—but I was going away from that airplane. None of the people bothered to follow me, as they were more curious about the airplane than they were about me. (Incidentally, the helmet and goggles I threw away in the pond were salvaged later by the man that owned the farm, Mr. Oberkamp, and he gave those back to me thirty-five years later when I went over to visit him. Mr. Oberkamp, unfortunately, died in the 1980s.) I went down the dirt road for a way, smelling worse, and finally came to a small stream or canal that passed underneath a bridge. I decided to go down and try to wash everything off. Unfortunately, it was to no avail. I was totally covered with cow manure to the extent that I could not wash it off of my flying clothes. These were heavy winter flying clothes—leather trousers and sheepskin-lined jacket, gloves, and boots, so I felt there was nothing to do but abandon the entire works on the spot, which I did. That was one of my big mistakes. Inside my trousers, in this flying suit, was my escape kit, which consisted of a compass, some money, a map, and other items that would have been valuable in trying to evade the enemy. Also, it left me with only a winter GI shirt, trousers, GI shoes and a light, leather A2 flying jacket. In February in Holland, that kind of clothing would be barely enough. One would freeze to death before too long, and I found this out in the next three or four hours.

"Looking back up the road, I could not see anyone following me, so I went into some woods and stayed there for the next three or four hours. I finally approached a farmhouse and watched two men working with some sugar beets for about thirty minutes to an hour before I decided that I had to make a move of some kind. It was by then late afternoon, and I was very, very cold. There was ice on the canals in the area, and it looked like it would start snowing almost any moment. So I decided to make a move.

"I waded the canal, which was about knee deep, and approached the two men. One of them looked at me very suspiciously when I told him I was an American pilot that needed some help, and I think the only word he understood was 'American.' The other man was a retarded individual, a very large man, and he was told by his friend, apparently, to watch me. The two men had been working with pitchforks in the sugar beets here, and the man who was retarded picked up the pitchfork and pointed it at me, while I was sitting on a big pile of sugar beets. I really didn't know what to expect, not knowing what country I was in anyway, so I reached around behind me and got a large sugar beet in my hand and held it, waiting to see what would happen. The other man went toward the house, and we sat there for a few minutes, until he finally came back and motioned me to come to the house, which I did. The people there offered me some food and hot drink and, not knowing who I was, they just motioned me to sit down and warm my feet, took my shoes off and my socks and put them near the stove so they'd get dry.

"This family did not speak any English, and of course I didn't speak Dutch or German. I still didn't know where I was until about thirty minutes later, when a young man about seventeen years old came in with one of the children of this family. The young man was William van Uem, and William had learned English in school. When he came in and spoke to me in English, I knew I was in friendly country. He told me where I was, about five miles inside Holland from the German border and near a town called Winterswik. He had a map, and pointed it out to me exactly. He told me the Germans were searching for me because they had seen the smoke and found the airplane, that they knew there was a pilot somewhere in the area, and that I must leave very, very shortly and try to get away from them, because if I was captured in the house—in that house or any other—the people would be dealt with very severely.

"All this I understood very well. So the family gave me an overcoat and a hat—a felt hat—and a pocketful of food which turned out to be heavy rye bread, very sustaining food, and sent me on my way. They pointed me toward the west, and there I went. As I left, it began to snow, and it was almost dark. Due to the exact location of this area it was necessary for me to walk due west in order to avoid the German border, which was not only to the east, but also on the north and on the south for some distance.

"I started out and used my very limited celestial navigation training in order to go west, keeping the north star on my right shoulder and the moon on my left shoulder. As it turned out, when I finally stopped two nights and two days later, I found out I had actually walked almost due west. During these two nights and two days, it snowed and sleeted most of the time. I waded several canals, and the fields were wet, so my feet were very wet and very cold all the time, and I did not have enough clothes on to stay very warm, except when I was moving. I would walk a while, get tired, and sit down, usually with my back to a tree someplace—it was too wet to lie down anyplace—and when I could stand no longer, I'd get up and walk some more. Once in a while I'd doze off and get maybe ten or fifteen minutes sleep, but not very much.

"After the first night and part of the day, I stopped walking for awhile. I was afraid to walk in the daytime anyway to any great degree. I found a barn that had been abandoned, about a hundred yards from a farmhouse, and it looked as though it were not in use constantly. I decided to stop there for awhile. This barn had a little bit of hay in the back, and that was about it. But at least it was dry on the inside, and I went in and sat down and tried to get a little sleep. In about an hour of so, a lady came down. She had seen me, and she had no idea who I was, but she knew there were a lot of fugitives around in the countryside from time to time.

"The people were very cautious, but still desirous to help anybody who really needed it. I think she took one look at me and decided I needed some kind of help, particularly after she looked at my shoes. She spoke to me only in Dutch, which I did not understand, but she seemed to think that I was all right. So she went to the house and brought me back a pair of wooden shoes, which I tried on. They were much too small, and I couldn't walk in them at all, but at least I could stick my feet in them and keep my feet dry for a little while. The lady brought me a little bread, and maybe some sandwiches. Obviously, she didn't have much to give. But she left me alone, and no one else came around at all that day.

"Just before dark that night, I started walking again, with the same routine, crossing the fields and canals, trying to steer a course due west the best that I could—of course, staying off the roads and staying away from the villages. I walked all that night, and the next day I holed up pretty much in the woods, walking very little. It was difficult to keep a straight course in daylight, because the sky was overcast most of the time and I didn't have enough sun to really guide me. At night it was much easier, with the stars, since the clouds were broken most of the time. So that night I started out again, and toward daylight the next day I decided that was as far as I could go without some help, warm clothes, and food.

"I saw a farmhouse and went into the barnyard area and lay down on a haystack. In that area, they stack their hay in a round stack with a roof on top of it to keep it dry. The roof comes down as they use it, but there's a little space between the roof and the hay, so I crawled in there to get some rest and get out of the weather. After a while, I heard some noise in the barn that was attached to the house. I went over and knocked on the door of the barn but received no response whatsoever, so I decided to move on.

"I walked about another three-quarters of a mile and came to another farmhouse. I walked into the backyard and heard a noise inside the barn. I knocked on the door, and a man came to the door and looked at me. I tried to tell him who I was. He didn't speak one word of English, but he did ask me to come inside the barn. We went on through the barn, where he had been milking, and into the house, where they motioned me toward the stove. Again, they could tell I needed my shoes and socks off to get warm and dry. They also gave me a little bit of breakfast and some hot milk.

"This man's name was Mr. Gosselink, and he had two boys and one little girl. He sent the two boys off to the gamekeeper's house to ask him what to do. A literal interpretation of what Mr. Gosselink told his boys to tell the gamekeeper was, 'I have something in my house and I don't know what it is. Will you please come and look.' With that, the boys took off in search for the gamekeeper. The gamekeeper did not come but instead sent a man whom he knew to be connected with the underground, and this man's code name was Bos. He came right away and talked to me at some length. Being a schoolteacher, he spoke very good English. Bos interrogated me to the extent that he was satisfied I was not a German spy trying to find out who was in the underground. This had been done from time to time, so they were very suspicious. However, after he had satisfied himself that I was not connected with the Gestapo or any other German organization, he told me he would do his best to get me out of there and down to Spain, which I had indicated to him was my goal.

"He left, came back with the gamekeeper and one other man, whose name is Spahnhoeck, a younger man about nineteen years old, and they took me to a small cabin in the woods not too far from Mr. Gosselink's dairy farm. This entire area was very near the town of Vorden, which held their post office, their governmental offices, train station, etc. The cabin had been built for a man who had been in the Dutch army when the war broke out and had been the area commander of that particular part of Holland. He was about sixty years old at the time, and finally the Germans took him captive and started him on the way to Germany. This gentleman escaped from the train, found his way back to the Vorden area, and the underground built him this cabin in the woods and kept him there for quite some time.

"He had since left and gone into hiding in another location. So they decided to put me in the cabin for the time being. The cabin was made for the most part of straw, with a wooden floor and a thatch roof—a flat thatch roof. It had a small, wood-burning stove, a small bench for a table, with a chair and a bed built into one end of it—the cabin being about six feet by six feet and about five and a half feet tall. I couldn't stand up straight inside the cabin, but when I went to bed, if I slept crossways I could stretch out all the way. The bed didn't have a mattress, but had straw on it, a cover over that, and the very top item was a polar-bear rug of some earlier vintage.

"I stayed in this cabin about forty-five days or so, and it snowed every day that I was there. The snow was quite deep all around, and that probably prevented curiosity seekers from finding where I was. Spahnhoeck was also hiding from the Germans and had an assumed name with a false passport. So he worked as a helper to the gamekeeper and would bring me something to eat every day about noon. He would also bring me wood. Then, one of the ladies who lived in the castle and whose family owned this particular large forest, would bring me something to eat every night.

"She was a very educated woman, she and her sister both, and she had many books in English. She would come, bring me something to eat, and we would talk for an hour or so. Then we would take a walk through the woods in the dark of the night. This lady at the time was somewhere around forty to forty-two years old, I would guess, and had lived all her life in these woods. She knew every little trail. When we went for a walk, she would walk in front of me. Though I could not see her at all, I could hear her and would follow her that way. We would walk for maybe a mile or a mile and a half through the woods covering many, many trails, but never getting outside of the woods and never getting near any house. She knew I needed exercise every day, because I was doing nothing else but sitting in the cabin, sleeping and reading the English books she would bring to me.

"After about forty-five days, Bos came to me and said that he'd made arrangements to take me to Amsterdam, where I could proceed farther with another segment of the underground. The gamekeeper dyed my GI shoes from brown to black, and stole a hat—a really nice derby hat—out of a barber shop someplace for me. They got me a stiff-collared shirt, some trousers, a nice over-coat, and a nice-looking tie. He dressed me up like a business-man of some prestige, money, and influence. They had also made me a fake passport, in case I was stopped. Spahnhoeck bought two tickets for us, and Bos and I started out for the train station in Vorden.

"En route, Spahnhoeck came by on his bicycle and handed us two tickets. When we arrived at the train station there were quite a number of people waiting for the train going to Amsterdam. So Bos stood at one end of the platform, and I at the other, reading a Dutch newspaper. I found out after a few minutes that I had the newspaper upside down, but apparently no one had noticed! Another part of my disguise was a box of very fancy cigarettes, the kind that the ordinary person could not afford, but which Germans in pretty high places could. There were occasions when Gestapo people and other Germans in civilian clothes would frequent places like the railroad station, or ride on the train from, say, Amsterdam into Germany and back. But most of them were of the type that even the Germans and the Dutch police didn't want to get entangled with. So they didn't bother to disturb them.

"Apparently, my disguise worked satisfactorily, and no one bothered to try to speak to me. Eventually Bos and I boarded the train, he sitting on one side, and me on the other, of the compart-ment, which held about six people. By the time the conductor came by to collect the tickets, it had turned dark, and the lights on the train were very, very dim, making it very difficult to see from one person to another. To avoid being drawn into conversa-tion with any of the people, I pretended to be asleep, and the conductor came in and shined his flashlight. He asked for tickets, and everybody gave him their ticket. So he spoke to me, but I had my eyes closed and didn't answer. He shined his flashlight in my face. Immediately I opened my eyes and realized it was the conductor and that he was taking up tickets. I gave him my ticket, everybody laughed, and he went on his way. After that no one disturbed me at all.

"Upon arriving in Amsterdam, another man met us. I was transferred from Bos to this other man and taken by streetcar and on foot to a family named Goedkoop. Jan Goedkoop was connected with the underground but was not the part of the group that ferried out Allied flyers on the run. He had a rather large house and had an extra room in it, so they put me up. The Goedkoops' household consisted of the man and his wife, Thea, and one daughter, Doicher, five years old, and a little boy, Jan Hymer, who was about eighteen months at this time. They were a very intelligent, very delightful couple that spoke about five languages, and both had been to England. She had studied there for about two years and had also studied in Switzerland with American and English girls for a couple of years, so it was very comfortable living there with them.

"After about five or six weeks at the Goedkoops' house, I was taken to another place across town, where a man and his wife and baby lived in an apartment complex. This man was a policeman, a Dutch policeman. He too was connected with the underground, but only to the extent that he would keep people in his house. And when I arrived, also staying there was a young airman of Italian extraction, a New Yorker. He had been a gunner on a B-17, had been shot down, and was living with them at this apartment.

"In my stay there, I saw my first and only real operation of the Gestapo. We were walking one night, early in the evening rather, down the street to get some exercise—the other GI, the man we were staying with, and myself—when we heard a woman screaming at the top of her lungs, and we ran down about a block to where we could see around the corner and find out what was going on. The policeman stopped us at this point, and we saw two or three Gestapo agents drag a man out of the front of his house and down the street. I asked the man we were staying with why she was screaming, and he told me they were Gestapo and that they were taking this man from his home, and the woman was screaming because she was quite sure she would never see him again. I'm sure he was right. The policeman had his gun with him, a pistol, but he didn't dare interfere with the Gestapo. They were deathly afraid of these people, and I can't say that I blame them very much.

"After about two weeks, I had decided that I was at a stalemate at this place and that I needed to do something to move on. When I decided to leave this particular apartment, I asked the young airman, the gunner, if he wanted to go with me, and he told me he was comfortable, he had plenty to eat, and he saw no purpose in leaving and going through any kind of exposure in order to get back to England. I explained to him that it was the duty of any man in uniform to get back to his own forces if he possibly could.

"I explained to our host that I wanted to move farther. Although he was very nice, very kind, and did everything that he could do for us, I didn't want to sit there any longer. So, I asked him if he would take me back to Jan Goedkoop's house, and he consented to do so. The trip back to Goedkoop's was uneventful in the streetcar, except for one small incident. The streetcar was very crowded, many people were standing, and I accidentally stepped on a lady's toe. Out of instinct, I turned around and said, 'Sorry.' But she nevertheless let me have a long piece of her mind in no uncertain terms, at which some of the people kind of laughed. This didn't bother me, but I thought maybe after I had said, 'Sorry,' that I had identified myself as an American. But I found out later that the Dutch used the same word under the same circumstances many, many times, without any difference in my pronunciation and theirs.

"We got off a couple of blocks from Jan's house and walked the rest of the way. When we knocked on the door, they greeted me with open arms. Upon my return, I found two other American flyers that had been shot down. One of them was a bomber copilot whose name escapes me. The other young man was Floyd Steger, a young fighter pilot from Illinois, about nineteen years old, who had been shot down about two or three weeks prior to this time.

"The Goedkoops were very nice people, but they could tell that I was very restless and that it was time for us to try to move on to our destination, which would have been Spain, and then back to England. Consequently, about two weeks after I had returned, they made arrangements for us to go to Maastricht, down in the southeastern part of Holland, adjacent to the Belgian border.

"For this trip Mrs. Goedkop's brother, Weinik Everts, who is still a good friend to this day, agreed to take us down to Maastricht. Weinik was in the underground, but he was in a different portion of the underground than the people who moved us about. Weinik's job, as was Jan Goedkoop's, was to get money and food stamps and false passports and that sort of thing to those people who needed them. Weinik, as well as Jan Goedkoop, was a unique individual who, while not large or very strong physically, managed to hold his own with the Germans. At one point, he was going across town on his bicycle with a lot of material on him, such as passports, that would have identified him as a member of the underground had he been caught. He was stopped by three German soldiers. These Germans were going to search him, and he knew that he couldn't allow this, so he threw his bicycle at one of them, punched another, and then ran.

"But the third man shot him in the back with a rifle, rupturing his spleen. Well, Weinik rounded the corner and ran into the first place he could find, which was one of the standard three- or four-story houses in that area, with a meat market in the lower floor. Weinik ran through the meat market, up the stairs, and onto the roof, telling the people not to tell that they had seen him, which they didn't. He lay on top of the roof all that night and the following day, and sometime late the next day he managed to get down and get in touch with Thea, his sister, and some other people, and made it over to her house, where she nursed him and kept him alive until he got well.

"Weinik took Floyd and me to the railroad station, where he bought our tickets, and we boarded the train for Maastricht. Weinik, of course, did not sit in the same compartment with us, in case we were caught. We had on our civilian clothes, had passports and identification papers, and we were all set to go—when two German soldiers came in and sat down in the same compartment with Floyd and me.

"They had their rifles with them. They were privates, but fortunately they didn't try to strike up a conversation. At on point, one of the Germans wanted to smoke a cigarette. He had no matches, so he asked me for a match. He asked me in Dutch. Fortunately, I knew that word, so it was no problem. I gave him a box of matches, and he lit his cigarette and handed them back. That was the end of our conversation with the two Germans, although they maintained a constant flow of talk between themselves the entire way. If I remember correctly, they got off the train just before our arrival in Maastricht.

"Naturally, Floyd and I were a little bit nervous about this situation. I had figured out what we were going to do if we got into trouble with them, and I suppose that Floyd had similar things in his mind, and that was to throw them out the window of the train (if we didn't get thrown out ourselves). There wasn't much else we could have done.

"Upon arrival at the Maastricht railroad station, Weinik met us and turned us over to another man who identified himself some way or another to Weinik, though they had never met. This gentleman took us on to the house of Dr. Van der Ley, and Weinik returned to Amsterdam. I would not see him again for about thirty-five years.

"Dr. Van der Ley was a doctor who had been practicing in Maastricht since he first got out of medical school. He was from the northern part of Holland, the Friesland area, primarily a Protestant area, whereas Maastricht is mostly Catholic. For this and other reasons, Dr. Van der Ley never did get along with most of the doctors in Maastricht and was never invited to join the local medical society or medical association. He was a rather large man and had been on the Dutch Olympic team in 1928 as a diver, and you could tell by his build even at that age—he was about forty to forty-five years old at that point—he was still in very good physical condition.

"Dr. Van der Ley's office was in the bottom floor of his house, which had three stories plus an attic. And on the bottom floor also was the dining room, the kitchen, and a very small parlor. Dr. Van der Ley's wife was Jewish and had been in a concentration camp for two or three years at the time that Floyd and I showed up, and the doctor was very, very bitter toward the Germans, naturally. He had his two bedrooms on the other two floors. The top bedroom, Floyd and I stayed in, and in the other bedroom were Dr. Van der Ley and his live-in nurse. In the attic was a radio that came from the United States Signal Corps. It was a low-frequency radio, used by a member of the Dutch underground who would come every day to send a weather report back to England.

"Dr. Van der Ley and I got in the habit of playing two-handed bridge—honeymoon bridge—each night. Floyd and the nurse, neither of whom played bridge, played checkers or read. The Doctor and I played bridge and usually ended up drinking from a bottle of Dutch Jeneva (which is gin) or cognac. We'd have one bottle one night, and the other the other night. We were equally fond of the stuff, although it was not the best brand and the alcohol content was not what it is today. We also listened to the BBC news each evening, so we were pretty well up on the air strikes.

Occasionally we'd hear the American and British bombers come over, and every day and every night we'd hear a few German aircraft flying by.

"The night before the invasion of June 6, 1944, Dr. Van der Ley and I were playing honeymoon bridge and drinking a bottle of cognac, when along toward midnight we began to hear more and more German planes coming across, going toward the west. We guessed immediately that the invasion was beginning. And sure enough, late that next evening on the BBC we learned that the Allied troops had landed in Normandy.

"For the next few days there was a tremendous amount of German activity in our area. About four or five blocks from Dr. Van der Ley's house was the local German Army (Wehrmacht) headquarters. And the street in front of his house was one of the main roads going from Germany and the northern part of Holland down to the Maas River, where there was a main bridge, and on down through Belgium into France. This was one route that was used quite heavily by a lot of German military traffic.

"About a week or so after the invasion of Normandy, Dr. Van der Ley went to town one afternoon and didn't come home that night for supper. I hadn't known him to do this before, but the nurse wasn't too surprised. Apparently, it had happened before when he'd go out and have a few drinks with the boys and wouldn't get in until eight or nine o'clock at night. But on this occasion he didn't come home at all. What had actually happened was that he had had a few too many drinks with the boys and found some German soldiers inside a pub where he was, and he decided he would whip the whole outfit!

"It took eight of them to corral him and take him down to the local jail, and that's where he spent the rest of the night. Early the next morning, the nurse received a telephone call from someone to the effect that Dr. Van der Ley was in jail and why he was there. So she knew immediately that the Germans would come very shortly to search his house. This was standard procedure under these circumstances. She called to warn the man who had been sending radio broadcasts back to England each day. She had told us to dress immediately and that we had to leave. The radio man arrived before we left, and buttoned up the radio equipment. This radio was portable and came in two cases, the entire outfit—everything you needed to set up a radio post, except the tower. It folded up just like two suitcases, but the suitcases were painted the old Army olive drab used in those days, and on the outside of each one was stamped 'United States Signal Corps.'

"This man folded them up, handed one each to Floyd and me, and we set out the front door. Fortunately for us that day, there was a funeral being held at a church across the street from Dr. Van der Ley's house. It was the funeral of a man who was very prominent and very well known in that area. The church and courtyard were full, the street was full of people, and people were backed up all along the sidewalk. From Dr. Van der Ley's house, one just opened the front door and stepped down onto the sidewalk. So, we stepped right into the crowd, following the radio operator, eased our way through the crowd and over to a side street without being unduly noticed, and started walking.

"Floyd and I didn't know where we were going, but the man stayed about a block ahead of us, and we followed him for several hours. We ended up beyond the edge of town, about a mile from the city limits, and we were taken into what they call the Caves, and these were literally caves.

"One more word about Dr. Van der Ley. He continually fed people like Floyd and me, flyers that had been shot down, as well as some people in the underground that had to stay in hiding, and some people who were actually starving. He would go out to the countryside and go to farmers whom he knew had vegetables, who cured a beef once in a while, or a hog, without letting the Germans know about it. He knew these people that had ample food, and he would make them fill up his sacks and his car, and he would bring the food back to feed the downed pilots and other needy people. No one knew what he was doing with the food, but they thought, 'My goodness, Dr. Van der Ley sure does have a lot of patients that need a lot to eat.' But they wouldn't say anything. They'd just give him the food and go on from there.

"After the war, it all came out—what he was doing with all this food, all the people he was hiding, not only in his house, but other places, and how he had taken care of so many people and literally fought the Germans in his own way throughout the war. He was decorated, as was Jan Goedkoop, with the highest civilian decoration given for wartime service by the American government, as well as by the British, the Dutch, the French, and the Belgian governments. In addition, there is a tree that was planted in a park in Jerusalem in honor of Jan Goedkoop, because of the work he did to save many, many Jews in hiding whom the Germans never did find in Amsterdam during the war.

"Dr. Van der Ley, after the war, was invited to join the local medical association, and you can imagine where he told them to go. 'Til the day he died, he never did change. He said, 'Uh-uh. You didn't want me then. I don't need you now.' Well, that's the way it goes.

"Back to the caves. These caves are quite famous in that area in that it's a network, several miles long, several miles wide, and inside the temperature is a constant sixty-five degrees. For several hundred years, the building materials for the forts, the churches, the walls, and bridge structures came from the sandstone walls of these caves. The Germans were afraid to go into them, because there were many, many tunnels running in all kinds of directions for many miles through the hills, and they'd sent patrols in there two or three times, and they never came out. To this day, one does not dare go in there without a guide.

"The underground had fashioned a very large room deep in there in which they stayed and operated. There were maybe two or three people at a time staying there constantly. They had some supplies, and you could build a fire if you wanted and do some cooking, and they had some places scraped out in the walls that would make a bunk. We were quite surprised, and quite pleased also, that we had such a secure place to stay for a while.

"Soon after the Normandy invasion began, all public transportation, as well as private transportation—there wasn't very much of the latter—was shut down by the Germans. In other words, there were no more passenger trains in occupied Europe. There were no buses, no streetcars, no automobiles, and very seldom even a bicycle. There were few exceptions. One was for trucks needed to haul food back and forth, what little food there was. It so happened it was one of these trucks that got Floyd and me across the border to Liege, Belgium.

"After just a few days, a truck came that was used to transport foodstuffs between Liege, Belgium, and Maastricht. It was owned and operated by a Belgian who was a part of the underground. This truck had a sheet metal roof on top, and it was enclosed entirely. They brought the truck into a garage-like place near the entrance to the caves, took off the top (the front part of the top) and rolled it back about two feet. Inside had been built a false partition between the back of the cab and the main part of the truck. It was behind this partition that Floyd and I rode on our way to Liege.

"They put us down inside. We could barely squeeze in, and we had nails sticking out all around us, and then they nailed the roof back on to the truck, and we set out for Liege. We were stopped at the border, of course, by the Germans, who opened the back door of the truck and looked inside. They came in and looked around. Then we heard the door close, and we proceeded on our way. Naturally, we had been briefed on this procedure and kept very, very quiet, barely able to breathe, until we got on the road again. When we came into Liege, the truck pulled into a garage, the doors were closed, the roof was taken off again, and we were taken out of there and kept for a few days in another halfway house.

"Finally, we were taken to live with a man and his wife in an apartment house in a far corner of town, almost out of town. There was a man in the Belgian underground named 'Roger,' who was in charge of the entire operation. He and I didn't get along very well from the beginning. After we had been at this man's apartment for a couple of weeks, Roger came out and visited with us one day, and I told him I was getting restless. The invasion was well along. The Allies had broken out of Normandy and were headed in the direction of Paris, and I felt that we had a good chance of hooking up with them if we could just get farther south, down toward Paris. At this point, Roger told me that he operated just like a Chicago gangster. He pulled a pistol out of his pocket, pointed it at me, and told me if I did anything to cause any of his people to be caught by the Germans, he would shoot me. Now, this didn't set too well with me, so I poked the gun aside (fortunately, he didn't pull the trigger) and told him that I thought that we'd just go on our way anyhow.

"Well, after a few more threats, he finally departed, and then I talked to the Belgian with whom we were staying. Of course, he was very nervous and didn't want any gunplay around. (Neither did I, for that matter.) But he really didn't know what to do. Finally, after a few days, I told him that I believed I'd just leave and walk toward the Allied lines, if I had to walk all the way to Paris. Floyd didn't know exactly what to do, but he decided he'd go along with me. So the two of us departed.

"This man's wife didn't have very much to cook. The fare was rather limited, but she did cook up a big batch of waffles, and Floyd and I stuffed our pockets full when we got ready to leave. Our host walked with us out to the edge of town, near the road that goes from Liege to Namur. Floyd and I departed Liege and started walking beside this road—not really beside it, just close enough to keep it in sight. Sometimes we were no more than a hundred yards from the road. Sometimes, we were as far as three-quarters of a mile. But we kept the road in sight to guide us.

"After two or three days, Floyd and I began to get a little weary and particularly a little hungry, because what waffles we hadn't eaten were beginning to get terribly stale—kind of like eating the shingles off of a house. One morning we woke up very early (we'd been sleeping on the ground out in the woods) and heard a lady singing 'On the Road to Mandalay' in English, at the top of her voice. We immediately got up and went to a fence separating the woods from an open field and saw this lady cutting across the field, still singing.

"I waved at her, and she came over to where we were. We conversed a few minutes in British (I mean in English—but hers was definitely a British accent), and she told us to follow her and that she would take us to get something to eat in a farmhouse. So we went with her to a farmhouse, where we got something better to eat and met the farmer who was the lady's husband (she had been a nurse with the British Expeditionary Force in World War I, had met and married this Belgian, and had stayed in Belgium ever since). When I asked him how he knew where we were, he said, 'We've been keeping our eyes on you for the last two or three days.'

"And they had. They had picked us out as rather suspicious characters, walking near the road, but in the woods, and of course they wondered who we were. They'd passed the word from farm to farm on down the road as we went along. So they'd kept an eye on us off and on for these days, not knowing whether we needed help or whether we were Germans in disguise. Later on, as the American Army swept up toward Liege, there were lots of German soldiers that changed into civilian clothes, and some of them were lures, of course.

"This farmer arranged to put us in a truck, and I don't know how he got the nerve to do so, but he hauled us for four or five miles—off onto a dirt road, down through a low-water ford across a river, and up to a place in the woods where he let us out. Incidentally, this truck was burning wood. It had a large wood-burning stove in the back that made, I suppose, methane gas, and this was pumped into the carburetor, and that's what the truck ran on. Not very efficient, but it was all the fuel they had.

"Floyd and I were dumped off by him, and there was a farmer who could not speak any English whatsoever, but we were told by the man who drove us to stay there and the farmer would take care of us. There was no shelter of any kind, just nothing but some woods, and there we made our camp, which consisted of a weather balloon that had probably been launched from England, had come down in that area, and had been salvaged by these people. The balloon was about eight by ten feet, made out of very heavy rubber, and served the purpose of a kind of ground cover, and that's what we had for a bed, with an old quilt for a coverlet.

"By this time it was I suppose mid to late July. Floyd and I had been there just a few days when a motorcycle arrived with two people on it, a priest and another American pilot, named Jules Blake. Jules had been shot down in a B-17 a few weeks earlier. He had been staying in Liege, and they brought him down to stay with us. That made three of us. The farmer brought us a jug of hot milk every morning, and then in the evening he'd bring us something to eat, usually some kind of stew.

"There was only one eventful happening during our stay in those woods. And that was a British airplane that came over one night and dropped a couple of men and a lot of supplies to a group of waiting underground people. They asked us to come along with them and run the radio for them, to talk to the pilot in this operation, which we did. The two men that came out with the equipment that was dropped were a Belgian sergeant serving in the British army and a British captain who was accustomed to this kind of work, probably a commando.

"At any rate, he had brought with him, in addition to explosives to blow up bridges, some weapons—mostly Bren guns made by the British. They asked us to help the Belgians in handling the weapons, to show them how to load them and so forth, which we did. Most of these underground people at this point were just farmers with no knowledge of weapons and no training whatsoever. They asked us to go with them on their escapade, blowing up bridges, among other things. After talking it over, Blake and I decided that wasn't the right thing for us to do, so we declined. Blake put it very bluntly. He said, 'If we get into a fight, there's going to be three of us standing there fighting, and the rest are going to run.' And that's just about what happened. The group was discovered a few days later by a German patrol, and the ones they didn't wound or kill all ran off and left their weapons behind.

"Somewhere around the middle of September, the Americans caught up with the Germans right in our area, and we were in the middle of an artillery duel, with Americans on one side of a hill, a couple of hills with a little river running through it, and the Germans on the other side. They were lobbing shells back and forth. It was quite obvious to everybody that the Germans were in pretty good retreat, and it would only be a matter of a few days before the American troops would overrun our area.

"Consequently, one night the farmer asked the three of us to come up and spend the night in the house, which we did. All of his family, plus a few neighbors, went down into the basement for shelter. The house was built out of heavy stone, and the basement was quite large and could accommodate all the people. But Floyd, Jules, and I discovered some feather beds up on the top floor, and that's where we decided to spend the night, regardless of the shells bursting and the windows rattling. We hadn't been in a bed in so long, we didn't care!

"The next morning, we had breakfast, and the farmer offered us the use of his razor to shave with. We hadn't had a decent shave in a long time, so I shaved my face with his straight razor, and then Blake was shaving. He was about halfway through when an American jeep with two GI's in it came roaring into the courtyard. We were so excited to see the jeep that Blake wiped the rest of the lather off and we stormed out the door, the three of us. These two GIs—a captain and sergeant—were with a 105mm artillery unit, I believe it was a battalion, that was from Patton's 3rd Army but had been attached to the 1st Army for their push up through that part of Belgium.

"A lady had gone to them where they had camped the night

before and told them about us, and so they said, 'We'll go get them.' It was about maybe a mile and a half from where we were to their encampment. So we immediately roared out of the court-yard, thanking the farmer and all the rest of them for their help, and took off down through the area (fortunately, we found a road) and back to their camp, where we had some American coffee, some American eggs, and I don't know what else. Of course, the eggs were powdered, and the men scrambled them, but they sure were good. We were glad to be there.

"After a few hours they took us to the headquarters of, I believe, General Hodges, Army Group II. At that point we were interrogated at quite some length by the Intelligence people there. Then we were sent to a camp, a prisoner of war camp, where the Americans were holding about five thousand German prisoners behind barbed wire. But our troops had some tents, and they had a mess hall that was quite nice, so we stayed there a couple of nights and then they put us on trucks to go to Paris.

"They were hauling prisoners as fast as they could back from the front lines, to some other place in France, and I think eventu-ally they were shipped to England or America. They put us on one of these POW trucks and sent us back to Paris, where the Red Cross gave us each a toothbrush and razor and whatever else they had, plus some fairly clean sheets that we were much obliged to sleep on.

"Paris had only been taken about two weeks before this, and the people were still showing the Tricolor, the French flag. Even the girls had made earbobs out of little pieces of tricolor material and stuck them on their ears, around in their hair, and so forth. In other words, Paris was still in a state of celebration when we ar-rived. Our clothes were pretty grubby, pretty bad, and we were in need of some clean clothes and clean bodies.

"After a couple of nights there, the Army put us on an air-plane and sent us over to England, where we were processed like many, many others. They were coming in almost daily at that point. They had set up a processing line to give us some clothes—a uniform, some money, that sort of thing. And then about a month later I was finally scheduled to fly from England back to the United States. I arrived back home somewhere around the latter part of October.

"I have been a member of an organization known as the 'Air Force Escape and Evasion Society' for a number of years. This organization is made up of men who were shot down in Europe in World War II and either escaped from the Germans or evaded them altogether. Practically all the members are evaders and owe their return to allied forces for the most part to the brave people of the Dutch, Belgian, and French underground. I had never attended a meeting of this organization until the meeting in Atlanta on May 21–25, 1986. There I was surprised to meet two men with whom I had been quartered in Liege, Belgium, in 1944, along with ten or twelve other downed fliers, including some from the RAF.

"I don't remember much about the house, except that no family lived there. The Belgians brought us food: I remember an elderly lady who came there each day to bring food and other supplies. I was there only three to five days. Anyway, as mentioned earlier, I got impatient and left, along with Floyd Steger.

"These two men I met in Atlanta remembered our leaving, and one of them, Lou Breitenback, had kept a diary of sorts and had my name and hometown (Rising Star, Texas) as well as Floyd's. The very day Floyd and I left this house, to be billeted with a private family, the others were picked up by the Gestapo, who had been watching the house. They became POW's for the duration of the war. Again I was lucky, but I didn't know it for forty-two years."

So ends the story of Colonel Alford's escape and evasion, as he wrote it.

14

1944

The new year began with a bang. President Roosevelt announced the appointment of Dwight Eisenhower as commander of all Allied Forces (replacing General Devers) for the invasion of the Continent. Ike in turn had Hap Arnold move Tooey Spaatz and Jimmy Doolittle to England to command the new U.S. Strategic Air Forces in Europe and 8th Air Force, respectively. They had headed his air arm in the North African campaign, and he wasn't about to change horses in midstream. Arnold sent Gen. Ira Eaker to Italy to command the Mediterranean Army Air Forces, which would include Nathan Twining's 15th Air Force, which had grown almost to the size of the 8th Air Force. It was a bitter blow to Eaker to have to step down after all he'd been through, having created the 8th Air Force Bomber Command from scratch, but it was the luck of the draw, mixed with a little military politics.

Doolittle's new strategy was direct: use our bomber force to attack the Luftwaffe's airfields, aircraft plants, aircraft industry; bring Germany's fighters up into the skies and then, with more aggressive 8th Air Force fighter support, wipe them out. The goal was for complete air superiority over the coast by the time of the invasion (first set for May 1944).

In late 1943, the arrival of the improved P-51 Mustang fighter made a great contribution to General Doolittle's goal of crippling German fighter defenses as well as their war industry. In its original design, the P-51 (a sleeker version of the Curtiss P-40) was underpowered by its Allison engine, could not climb, and was considered by the experts at Wright Field to not have any long-range escort ability.

But in 1942 the British, who had used the plane for strafing attacks in the desert campaign, substituted Rolls-Royce engines in five of their P-51s, with terrific results. In the United States, this led to the installation of Packard-built, supercharged Merlin engines in the P-51, which could then reach 440 miles per hour in the thin air of thirty thousand feet. By 1944, the long-range P-51 was able to escort our bombers deep into Germany and back.

Our 92nd group briefed twelve missions and flew eight of them during January. Weather prevented us from flying the other four. But the biggest and best happening of the new year was the arrival of the new, long-range P-51 fighters. Though we did not yet have them in great enough numbers, we did have some coverage all the way to the target, and a bomber with an engine out or other damage now had some hope and help against the Luftwaffe. As the long-range fighter numbers grew, we saw some massive air battles and, between our bomber attacks on German aircraft factories and airfields and the aerial combat and ground-strafing attacks by our new, long-range fighters, we could see the German Luftwaffe being slowly decimated.

One day in January our group received a message from 8th Air Force Headquarters that officers who had finished a combat tour would be given a thirty-day leave in the United States—if they would agree to come back for a second tour. I jumped at the opportunity, for I felt it might be my only chance to get back home, even for a short period. Besides, I could see that we were winning the war and, with the added long-range fighters and the coming invasion of the Continent, a second tour would be duck soup compared to my first. I placed my request before Colonel

Reid the next day, and he approved it with a smile. I flew my twenty-fifth and last mission of my first tour as deputy air commander on a comparatively easy raid on Chateaudun on February 5, 1944.

In late February 1944, I finally received my orders to proceed on or about March 25 to the port of Liverpool for my trip home. I was ecstatic. I'd only been home for one weekend since joining the Air Corps in 1941. My old friend Capt. Blair Belongia flew me to Liverpool on the appointed day for the first leg of my homeward journey.

The next day I boarded the USS *West Point* with one hundred highly decorated Army Air Corps officers, all of whom had finished combat tours, and fifty to sixty U.S. Army nurses, all of whom were pregnant and wearing wedding rings.

The returning group of officers were some of the 8th Air Force's best, including Lt. Col. Dave Schilling and Walker Mahurin, both aces of Hub Zemke's famous 56th Fighter Group. (It took at least five confirmed combat kills to qualify as an ace.) Capt. Joseph L. Egan Jr., my roommate aboard ship, whom I had met the year before while shooting film for William Wyler, was also an ace. Also on board were Maj. Larry Dwyer of the 91st Bomb Group and Capt. Fitzgerald of the 95th Bomb Group. All these fellows were fun people and interesting to talk to.

The ship was empty except for us, which made our voyage a very restful and enjoyable one. We spent the days playing poker and checking out the nurses, none of whom were much interested or interesting. The voyage home was uneventful, but the arrival in New York was spectacular. We docked at about 7 P.M., and darkness had fallen, but all the lights in New York were on, and I hadn't seen a light at night for eighteen months. I couldn't get over how the place sparkled.

Then came an announcement that only field-grade officers could disembark that night. My roommate, Capt. Joe Egan, was devastated. He wanted to go into town so much. I solved his problem pronto. I handed him two of my major's leaves and told him to pin them on his tunic and to come on. We were going to town.

We walked all around midtown Manhattan, stopping in a bar or two for drinks. We couldn't get over all the bright lights. Finally he said, "What do you want to do tonight?" I answered that I had nothing special in mind. He said, "Well then, why don't you come over to my house?" I asked, well, where was his house? He modestly said, "Oh, just over here on Park Avenue." His house turned out to be that of his parents, a beautiful ten- or twelve-room townhouse.

His parents were excited to have him home and were most cordial to me. Joe's wife and baby arrived shortly, and they had a big reunion. After some late dinner his father turned to me and said, "What can we do for you?" I answered that I'd been trying to get through to my girlfriend in West Virginia but couldn't get a line. He said, "I can fix that." He picked up the phone, called someone, and handed me the phone, saying, "Here you are—just tell them who you're trying to reach." He was an executive of the Western Union Company and obviously had some clout with the telephone folks. It was shortly after midnight when I called my college sweetheart, whom I hadn't seen for nearly two years, and let her know I was in New York and asked her to marry me. With her great sense of humor she responded by saying, "You'd better come down here and look me over before you jump into matrimony. After all, you haven't seen me for two years, and I might not look the same." I said, "I'll take my chances, set the date."

En route home I stopped in Richmond to visit Jack and Cora Francis Blair. Jack had been my roommate in college, and I had been their best man in 1941. He was now a major in the Aviation Engineers based at what today is the Richmond Municipal Airport at Sandstone, Virginia. I also purchased a new summer uniform for my coming wedding.

After greeting my parents I told them of my impending wedding, which had been set for May 11 (it now being about April 25).

My mother was aghast, saying, "I just cannot get ready that quickly." My father laughed, and I said, "Mom, get started now. I can't have you late for my wedding."

On May 11, 1944, I married Miss Constance Bailey of Bluefield, West Virginia, the prettiest redhead I'd ever seen. Since I was able to squeeze only thirty-five gallons' worth of gasoline stamps from my local rationing board, our honeymoon was a local affair that included the Cascades Inn at Hot Springs, Virginia, a trip to Richmond to meet Lt. Betty Copenhaver, a Wave officer who had been my wife's roommate at West Virginia University, and then and back home.

It was near midnight on the evening of our wedding when we arrived at the Cascades Inn. There was no one around except the desk clerk, and we assumed that due to the war there just weren't many guests in the hotel. The following morning we slept late, and as we descended the stairs to the dining room for breakfast, we were greeted by a room full of hotel guests lining both sides of the corridor, throwing rice upon us. They seemed so ancient-looking to me, for I was twenty-five and they were fifty-five or more. We all had a good laugh, and they greeted us with much good humor. A few days later Lt. Betty Copenhaver, who was stationed in Norfolk, Virginia, met us at the John Marshall Hotel in Richmond. We had a grand visit, but there was a mixup in her reservation that was finally resolved by the hotel's putting a cot in our room. I thus became one of a very few men who slept with two pretty girls on his honeymoon.

Our affair lasted almost forty-eight years, until Constance's death in 1993. She was the greatest, just a super woman.

Upon our return to combat, Joe Eagan was killed while on a strafing mission.

In late May 1944 we were ordered to report to Atlantic City to begin our journey back to England. We all took our wives to the Air Force Redistribution Center there and had an extra two weeks of vacation. Then the order came for us to report to New York City, sans wives, for our return to England.

We spent another enjoyable two weeks in New York await-
ing a ship assignment. During this time the Republic Aviation
Corporation, which had developed and built the P-47 fighter air-
plane, entertained us royally—for Lt. Col. Dave Schilling, Walker
"Bud" Mahurin, and the 56th Fighter Group had all made their
P-47 famous.

Finally, we were given full field equipment, including gas
masks, and put aboard the Queen Mary, along with an entire Infantry division and selected other units, for our voyage. Sixteen
of us occupied one stateroom, sleeping in tiered cots about thirty
inches apart. Someone told me that we had twenty-one thousand
troops on board.

The voyage back was terrible. The weather was not too bad,
but it seemed to me that the troops were seasick all the time. We
were given two meals a day, and I was assigned to a table with
two infantry majors who hadn't been at war yet. After our first
meal of the day I would always make myself a couple of sandwiches from the leftovers and stick them in my pocket. The two
majors looked at me as if I'd committed some disgraceful social
blunder. By the third day I noticed that they too were stuffing
sandwiches in their pockets. They were learning their first survival lessons.

I arrived back at my group at Podington about a week after
D-Day. The activity at Operations was unbelievable. The group
was flying several missions each day in support of the Allied
armies. Bombardment squadron strength had been increased to
about twenty-four airplanes and thirty-four aircrews. Each squadron was now flying at least two sorties a day, sending twelve
ships to a target in the morning and twelve again in the afternoon. With daylight lasting until nearly midnight, there were even
some sorties flown in the evening.

Nearly all of these support raids were easy because they were
such short missions and were rarely over enemy territory. They
were referred to as "milk runs" and everybody wanted on them
because they were so easy and safe. Along with these missions

we also had several raids on what were code-named "No Ball" targets, which were the sites from which the German V-2s were being fired. Because they too were very close to the coast they also were easy missions. It was a strange sight to approach the V-2 areas at twenty-five thousand feet and watch the white ribbons of condensation trails from those rockets, rising vertically in front of you straight into the heavens. Sometimes it appeared that they might fly right through our formations.

Though these missions in support of the invading armies were easy to fly from a safety standpoint, they often were very difficult because of target identification problems. These targets could be rock quarries, orchards, or crossroads, frequently in areas beyond the smoke markers. All too often they were difficult to pick out through the haze and smoke, and unfortunately we killed some of our own troops on two or three occasions.

Shortly after I returned to my job in Group Operations, my boss, Lt. Col. Robert Keck, was reassigned to the States and I was promoted to his position as the group's operations officer. I soon brought in as assistants Capts. Edgar Worth of Pasadena, California, and John T. Benedict of Chicago. Both had finished their combat tours and provided the help we needed to keep up with the great increase in operational activity. We were now briefing missions almost every day and dispatching hundreds of airplanes per month. Soon, our four operational squadrons added more airplanes and air crews and had twenty-five airplanes and about thirty-six crews each. Our groups were now sending out as many as four eighteen-ship groups in one day, as was every other group in the 8th Air Force. Our bomb tonnage per raid had quadrupled. We were now able to hit several targets in one day, and 8th Fighter Command, having almost eliminated the German fighter forces, was now strafing every train, boat, truck, car, and anything else that moved in daylight behind the German battle lines.

Allied troops now almost never had to worry about attacks from the air, for between the U.S. and British Air Forces we had airplanes above our ground troops nearly all the time. Our B-24s were transporting gasoline to Patton's 3rd Army when he was advancing faster and farther than the Army transports could supply him.

15

Headquarters

Prior to being transferred to Group Operations, I'd always been a squadron flying officer and socialized entirely with my squadron mates. After I was transferred to Group Headquarters, I continued to join my old squadron friends at the officers' mess for lunch and dinner. Colonel Reid one day very pointedly explained to me that I was now a part of the Group Headquarters Squadron and was expected to sit at the Headquarters table at mealtimes. I didn't relish having to eat or even associate with the Headquarters officers, for most were not flying officers and nearly all of them were ten or more years my senior. I thought of them as old men. I was twenty-five years of age, and they were in their mid thirties.

One of these officers was Maj. Marshall T. Boone, our provost marshal. He was a huge man, about six foot five, had thick glasses, and wore a raccoon topcoat most of the time. He had a slightly officious personality in the view of us younger officers, for he always acted as if he knew more than we did on almost any subject that we might bring up. Some of us younger officers, who were new in the headquarters, began to resent Major Boone, and we began to try to come up with some little known subjects for dinner table discussion that he would not know about.

Someone suggested we discuss football, and one of us brought up some statistics on Frankie Albert, the great Stanford quarterback. Quickly, Major Boone corrected him, saying, "Boys, you've got that wrong." One of us replied, "Now Major, how do you know anything about Frankie Albert?" "Well, hell," he said, "I played tackle on the same Stanford team with him from 1928 to 1931."

Someone suggested anthropology, and we briefly discussed it among ourselves before going to dinner one evening. At the appointed moment we launched into our discussion, including the findings in Siberia of certain artifacts from the diggings there. Major Boone immediately spoke up and said, "No boys, you have that wrong too." And we quickly asked how he'd know anything about that. Then with an all-knowing smile he said, "Well, I spent the entire year in 1932 with Professor So-and-so of Stanford University in Siberia digging up those things."

With that we gave up. We grudgingly recognized that he simply knew more than we. There was no way we twenty-five-year-olds could outwit this old major.

On another occasion, I was leaving to go to London on a three-day pass. He saw me and asked me where I was going. I told him to London for three days. He yelled back and said, "Wait a minute! I'll see if I can get a pass and go with you." I hoped he wouldn't get permission, for the last thing I wanted to do was to go to London with this old fellow. He soon came running out with his overnight bag, and we headed to town.

En route, he asked me where I intended to stay. I answered that I supposed I would stay in the Red Cross Club. "Oh," he said, "Let's stay in a hotel." I said, "Now Major, you know without a reservation we'll never get into a hotel." "Ah," he said, "Just leave it to me, I'll get us in." I quietly thought that this old goat was full of hot air, he'll never get us in any hotel, for by July of 1944 London was teeming with soldiers, and every hotel and bar was jammed.

When we got off the train, Major Boone grabbed a cab and

asked the driver to take us to the Savoy Hotel, one of London's finest. When we arrived the lobby was crowded, and when we got to the front desk Major Boone told the clerk he'd like a suite. The clerk asked if he had a reservation, and he answered that he did not. The clerk replied, "Sorry, we're full up." With that, Boone asked him to get the assistant manager. Shortly, a rather small man wearing a swallow-tailed coat appeared and addressed Major Boone, saying, "Sir, what can I do for you?" Boone replied that he was Major Marshall T. Boone of the U.S. Army Air Corps and that he wanted a suite. The manager asked if he had a reservation, and when Boone said that he didn't the manager said with a sneer, "Sorry Major, we're full," and turned to walk away. With that, Boone reached across the counter and grabbed the manager by the shoulder, spun him around, and said, "Sir, you didn't understand me, I am Maj. Marshall T. Boone, a member of the firm Boone and Boone in Baltimore, Maryland. We hold the mortgage on this damned hotel and, by God, I want a suite." With that we got a seven-room suite complete with baskets of fruit and wine! I couldn't believe it.

For the next three days, Boone sat in the suite and drank whiskey while I took in the shows and enjoyed some fine dining and some London clubs that I belonged to. When the time came to return to Podington, Major Boone was unable to navigate. He hadn't shaved for three days and was a mess. I managed to get him up, shaved him, and packed his bags. I escorted him to the elevator, with him on one arm and both our bags under the other. When the elevator doors finally opened, out came two very young lieutenants. Major Boone, in his now very low and graveled voice, said, "Boy, you got a room?" The lieutenant replied he didn't, "Boy, you got any whiskey?" The reply was again, "No sir." "Well," Boone said, "You got girls?" and again the lieutenant replied he did not. Major Boone said, "Son, you see that door standing open there, it's yours for as long as you want to stay."

Several months later, Major Boone sat us all down one

evening and said, "Boys, back in Baltimore before the war I was a stockbroker, and I know something about stocks and the stock market. I've been watching the London Stock Market, and I've noticed that Royal Dutch Shell Oil Company is selling for around sixpence a share. Now, that's because the Japanese have taken over all their Far East holdings. If we lose the war your money isn't going to be of any value anyway, but if we win the war Shell is going to get all their holdings back and will again be a viable, growing company. Now, you young fellows have been going to London and throwing your money away on $80 per bottle whiskey and girls, and after the war you're going to need some money. I advise you to buy yourselves a few thousand shares of Shell at a cost of maybe 50 pounds and lay it away for later."

I, of course, at twenty-five years of age was far too smart to follow this old major's advice. But the first time after the war I looked at Shell's price on the New York Stock Exchange it was $42 a share, or 420 times what it cost in 1944! I never saw Marshall Boone after the war, but I did talk with him by phone on two occasions, trying to get him to attend reunions of our old 92nd Bomb Group.

Another character at Headquarters was Mellor W. Stevenson of Cleveland, Ohio. Mellor was another six-foot, five-inch, two-hundred-fifty pounder who had been an aide to Gen. George C. Marshall in Washington in 1942. He was young, just out of Washington and Lee University, full of vim and vigor, and understandably bored in a Washington office. He had asked General Marshall to send him to Europe, and he was assigned to our group.

I first met Mellor in the spring of 1943. He asked me where I was from, and I told him Charleston, West Virginia. He then asked if I knew Joe Littlepage. I answered yes, that I knew the entire family and that in fact I had been named for Joe's father, Mr. Kemp Littlepage Sr. With that he said, "Well, I'm moving in with you, because Joe is my best friend, and anyone who is a friend of Joe's is a friend of mine." He'd gone to Kentucky Military Institute with Joe and then had played football at Washington and Lee with him. They were fast friends. Unfortunately, Joe was killed flying a B-24 in the Pacific.

Mellor Stevenson was full of humor and loved to have a few drinks and play practical jokes on his friends. He masked these playboy characteristics with great military bearing and could be all business when he felt it necessary.

One Saturday night, when we had been "stood down" by the 8th Air Force Headquarters, which meant we would not fly the next day, Mellor and I and four other officers borrowed a lorry and drove over to the 384th Bomb Group to a Saturday night officers' dance. Among our group was Lt. Bill Dace, of Oklahoma, who, when he had too much to drink, could not speak. He would simply utter an "Ugh" sound and shake his head yes or no. The new commander of the 384th Group was Col. Dale Smith, who had been on the U.S. Military Academy boxing team and had recently replaced Col. Budd Peaslee as the 384th Group commander.

We all went into the bar at the 384th officers' mess and ordered drinks. I don't exactly know how it all began, but quickly Mel Stevenson was confronting Col. Dale Smith for hitting Lieutenant Dace. It seems that Dace could no longer speak, and Colonel Smith had had enough to drink to want to spar a little, and Dace happened to be standing next to him. Colonel Smith was about six feet, six inches tall, with an exceptional reach. He had invited Lieutenant Dace to box a round with him, and when Dace only said, "Ugh," Colonel Smith put his left arm around Dace's head and began to hit him. Stevenson, who was standing nearby, grabbed the colonel's arm and pulled him away from Lieutenant Dace, who was now slumping to the floor with another "Ugh." With that, Smith turned to Captain Stevenson and said, "You're more my size. Come on outside and we'll have a match."

I was at the other end of the crowded room and knew nothing about this ruckus until someone came to get me. When I got to the door I could hear Stevenson yelling, "Hey Mac, hey Mac! Come here and help me!" I ran out to where a crowd had gathered, and there was Stevenson sitting on Colonel Dale Smith's chest, with his hands on each of Smith's arms, holding him flat on his back on the ground. He couldn't afford to let him up, for he'd have to fight him if he did, and he didn't know what to do next, it being a little unusual for a captain to fight a colonel. I quickly sent one of our officers to get our lorry and retrieve Lieutenant Dace, and, with Stevenson jumping aboard, we left for home without further ado.

The next morning, Colonel Reid called us on the carpet for a full confession of our Saturday-night activities. We gave him a full report, and he told us not to leave the base until the 40th Combat Wing had interviewed us. We heard no more of this incident, and we never again attended a 384th Bomb Group party.

Later, Mellor Stevenson came to work in Group Operations as base training officer. Immediately our group began to report huge increases in training hours, particularly in aircraft identification, a very important subject since we'd been told to expect sneak strafing and bombing attacks from the Germans at anytime. Soon we were leading our entire 1st Air Division in identification training hours. We had also achieved excellent bombing results and were leading in that all-important category. General Williams, our division commander, paid us a visit to commend us on our good work. At lunch he asked how in the world we had been able to do so much aircraft recognition training. His question was passed down to Captain Stevenson, and he replied, "Well sir, we have at least five hundred to one thousand men working outside all day, every day, and there are airplanes flying across our field every few minutes, and everyone on the field stops to watch the airplanes fly by. So I calculate that the one thousand men on the average look at airplanes an average of one and one half hours every day. That's twenty thousand hours per month." General Williams smiled. Colonel Reid looked as if he'd dropped his teeth and abruptly changed the subject.

Later that summer Colonel Reid was hospitalized for combat injuries, and Lt. Col. Andre Brousseau, our group executive officer, took command in Reid's absence. He was in the class of 1940 at the U.S. Military Academy and was bucking like hell to make chicken (full) colonel. He immediately began to shape up our group in every respect and demanded more and more of everyone.

In the meantime, someone at 8th Air Force Headquarters decided that everyone should start buying war bonds and set a quota for each division, which in turn set one for each group. Colonel Brousseau, ambitious to impress General Williams, began to put the pressure on all of our squadron commanders and all officers to chip in generously and oversubscribe our quota. There was terrible bitching and griping, because none of us felt that those fighting the war should have to buy war bonds. But since this was the military, we had no choice, so we did oversubscribe our quota, and Colonel Brousseau was very happy.

Mel Stevenson called me into his office and said, "Mac, let's play a joke on Colonel Brousseau." With that he muffled his voice with some towels and paper stuffed around the phone and called the colonel's office next door, saying that he was General Williams' aide at 1st Division Headquarters and that he was calling at General Williams's request to commend and thank Lieutenant Colonel Brousseau for doing such a splendid job selling war bonds under such unpopular circumstances. He told him that General Williams was really happy and thought Brousseau had done a great job.

That day at lunch Brousseau told us all about his call from General Williams and how happy he was, and thanked us all for having helped him with this problem. I knew right then that Stevenson and I were in trouble. After dinner that evening, Stevenson and I went down to the hospital to visit Colonel Reid and told him about the joke we had played on Brousseau. He laughed for ten minutes and thought it was the greatest thing he'd heard. After we left the hospital Colonel Brousseau called, and Colonel Reid began kidding him about his call from General Williams and then leaked the truth to him as to what we'd done.

The next day Stevenson and I were confined to the base and told that no leaves for either of us would be approved until further notice. We were really in the doghouse. After a few days, he relented, but we knew not to try any more jokes.

In the spring of 1943, when many American boys who had joined the Royal Canadian Air Force were transferred to the U.S. Army Air Corps, a young RCAF flying sergeant, whom the RAF had trained to be a navigator, was commissioned as a flight officer and transferred to our group. He was Howard F. Eaton, whom we called Tim, and he turned out to be at least one of the best navigators in the 8th Air Force. He had been flying British torpedo bombers (Beauforts) and had gained quite a lot of navigation experience. The British apparently stressed target identification more than we did, and that was one of the most important phases of a bombing mission.

Tim was assigned to Capt. Blair Belongia's crew, and they soon became a lead crew. Tim was such an outstanding navigator that most of the time, when Colonel Reid would fly as air commander leading our 1st Air Division or the entire 8th Air Force, he would insist on flying with Flight Officer Eaton. Timmy would nearly always get you to the Initial Point on time and help the bombardier identify his target in plenty of time to get the ship lined up properly and the rest of the ships in tight formation for a good bomb pattern.

As good as he was as a navigator, Tim was a little deficient in his deportment. He was very young, maybe nineteen or twenty years old, and wild as a March hare. He was a small fellow of about five feet, six inches with blue eyes, rosy cheeks, and blonde hair. He didn't appear to be more then fourteen or fifteen years of age and looked like a choir boy. He always carried a smile on his face and a twinkle in his eyes. The English lasses loved him, and he returned their affection with great passion. On one occasion when we were having a Saturday night dance, Lt. Hubert Miller, whom we nicknamed "Goon" because of his size (he played tackle for Clemson University), lost his date. He looked high and low for her, and he'd finally gotten himself a fresh drink and was leaning on the piano behind the band with a look of disgust on his face. It was rather dark in the corner behind the piano. I walked up and was chatting with him when suddenly he looked down behind the piano and said, "Well, I'll be damned." He reached over and with one hand lifted Tim straight up by his belt and pushed him through a nearby open window. Tim had been pursuing Goon's date in the dark behind the band. We never let either of them forget that incident, for they were the butt of several jokes thereafter.

Tim went on to lead many missions, earning several decorations and becoming a great asset to our group. I tried on two or three occasions to put through a promotion for Tim, but each time he'd manage to have too much to drink and start a fight and blow it. Captain Belongia, his pilot, and I were good friends, and one day he told me his squadron commander was sending his crew to southwest England for a week's vacation. I called Major Word, his commander, and told him that if he'd prepare Tim's promotion papers I'd walk them through and try to get Colonel Reid to sign them. He agreed because he too liked Timmy. I personally took Tim aside and told him what we were doing and told him that if he'd straighten up and watch his conduct I'd get him promoted. He was all for it and promised me that he'd be careful.

When I took his promotion papers to Colonel Reid for his signature he laid them on his desk and told me to have Captain Belongia's crew report to him before they departed. I sent his message to Belongia, and at the appointed time I accompanied them to Reid's office. They reported to the Colonel's office and stood at attention in front of his desk. Colonel Reid greeted them and expressed his desire for a happy vacation for them. Then turning to Timmy, he said, "Flight Officer Eaton, Mac [meaning me] has brought me these papers and asked me to sign them appointing you a second lieutenant in the United States Army Air

Corps. I am not going to sign them today, but if you go on this week of leave, and stay out of trouble, I'll sign them when you return." Eaton thanked him profusely and promised his best conduct. The crew saluted and departed for the train station for the first leg of their trip. It was about 12 noon.

About 4 P.M. our headquarters received a call from a small town about ten miles down the road. Timmy had gotten off the train at the first stop, had gone into a pub, and had somehow incited a riot between some U.S. Army Engineer troops and a group of black soldiers from a truck battalion! The British bobbies had arrested him, and we had to send our provost marshal to retrieve him. Needless to say he remained as Flight Officer Eaton for some time.

On August 26, returning from a raid on Gelsenkirchen, Germany, Colonel Reid was injured when a flak burst near the plane hit him in the legs. As described earlier, he was hospitalized for nearly a month and never again flew in combat. He was relieved of command and returned to the States in October.

"Darky " Reid was an unusual commander. Unlike most, he was so laid back, with so much humor, one would never suspect that he was a combat group commander. He knew all the senior Air Corps officers by their first names. One day he received a call that Col. Anthony "Tony" Mustoe, the new 1st Division inspector, was on his way to inspect our base. Colonel Reid dispatched me to meet Colonel Mustoe at the base gate and bring him directly to Reid's quarters.

I did meet Mustoe and escorted him straight to Reid's quarters. Reid greeted him with open arms and fixed him a drink of Scotch whiskey. Soon after, with me driving the staff car, Reid took him around the base, never letting him out of the car, and delivered him back to the front gate with a hearty goodbye, saying, "Now you've seen our base. Write what you will." Mustoe was furious but went along with the joke.

A few weeks later, Col. Curtis E. LeMay was promoted to

commander of the 3rd Air Division, and Colonel Mustoe was given command of LeMay's 305th Bomb Group. The 305th Group shortly began to decline in bombing accuracy, airplane maintenance, and overall was falling apart.

General Williams again sent Colonel Mustoe to visit Reid to learn how to run a bomb group. Again I accompanied Reid as he took Tony Mustoe around our base. He needled him for the first few minutes as we drove around, saying, "Tony, that's an airplane," as we passed one, "that's a truck, that's a hanger," as if Tony hadn't seen one before. But he spent three days with us and then returned and successfully ran the 305th Group. The truth was any organization would have suffered when it lost a strong commander like Curtis LeMay, as the 305th had.

Colonel Reid had instructed me to bring each new air crew to his office before they flew a mission, because he said he wanted to meet them all, for very likely some would be lost on their very first mission. Reid was from Georgia, and when I would introduce him to new pilots he would always ask them where they were from. If they answered Georgia, he would invariably ask them where in Georgia, and they would always say Atlanta. Then with a big grin he'd say, "Now son, tell me where in Georgia you're really from." With that, the young officer, with reddened face, would admit to being from some small town. Reid would always say, "Don't let it bother you son, everyone from Georgia always says they're from Atlanta."

On another occasion, when our group's airplanes were lined up on the takeoff runaway awaiting the takeoff flare signal, the 8th Bomber commander called us to tell the air commander to change the route at a certain point. Radio secrecy being a must, we had to write the message out and hand carry it to the lead airplane. The high squadron was lined up in first position for takeoff, followed by the group lead airplane and its lead squadron, with the low squadron being last. All of the airplanes were warming and checking their engines at about fifteen hundred to eighteen hundred rotations per minute. With twenty-one air-planes, each with all four engines running, a huge wind storm was taking place on that runway and around the lead airplane.

It was pitch dark as I drove Colonel Reid out to talk to the air commander and explain the message. I pulled up near the wing tip of the lead airplane, and Reid got out to walk to the front belly hatch, located just a few feet in front of the number two propeller. With the tail wheel on the ground, the tips of the propellers were only about three and a half feet above the pavement, and the wash began to pull him back toward the propeller. As he struggled to regain his balance, he kept trying to rise. He missed the whirling propeller by an inch, finally grabbing the horizontal stabilizer on the tail, and crawled away from the propeller wash. I held my breath as he passed under that propeller. He then motioned the pilot to reduce power and walked to the hatch on the second try.

Col. William M. "Darky" Reid retired from the U.S. Air Force in 1956. He was the best pilot I had ever flown with, and I was certain he'd be the last ever to die in an airplane. He was killed during an instrument approach into New Orleans.

In late September, Lt. Col. James W. Wilson was assigned as our new group commander. He was a class of 1939 U.S. Military Academy graduate and had first arrived in England in 1942, as a squadron commander in the 306th Bomb Group. In early 1943, his airship caught fire during an attack and he was badly burned. He had been sent back to the States to recuperate and had somehow talked his way back into the 8th Air Force.

He was smart and ambitious enough to have set his sights on becoming chief of the entire Air Force. He set out to make the 92nd Bomb Group the best in the 8th Air Force. He immediately began to relieve all of the older officers and replaced them with a group of bright, younger officers. Lieutenant Colonel Wilson was very demanding and began pressuring all commanders to clean up their areas and paint their buildings, and he expected our operational squadrons to fly the tightest formations of any group. His insistence on formation flying resulted in two major midair collisions, though no lives were lost.

He pushed formation flying to the point that the squadrons were distracted from emphasizing hitting the target, and accuracy began to drop until we were near the bottom in this category. I warned him that we must keep hitting the target as our first priority, but he paid me little heed.

Late one afternoon I got a call from General Williams, our division commander. He said, "Mac, what's wrong up there at your group, you're slipping badly." I answered that the top emphasis was on formation flying now. He then said, "You go find Wilson and tell him to report to me immediately."

About 5 P.M. that evening, I told Colonel Wilson of the general's request, and he immediately left for the forty-five-minute drive to Division Headquarters. At about 7 P.M. I was in the lobby of the officers' mess when he returned. He said, "Mac, go get the four operational squadron commanders and the group navigator and bombardier and tell them to report here immediately for a meeting."

That night Wilson gave us a pep talk on the importance of getting bombs on the target. He'd received a good warning from General Williams and was now ready to make hitting the target our number one priority. All the squadron commanders who had worked so hard to get us into first place in bombing results looked at each other with knowing smiles.

Colonel Wilson's efforts, however, began to pay off in many ways. He was far more progressive and aggressive than our previous commanders. Our base began to look neater and cleaner, with all hands paying more attention to their duties than before. About this time he ran a contest for a motto for our group. The final selection was "Fame's Favored Few"—a name that stuck.

He brought in Lt. Col. "Rip" Riordan from the 306th as our group executive officer. Rip had earned quite a reputation as a combat leader. He also promoted Mel Stevenson to the position of ground executive officer. New faces with new brooms.

On November 29, Jim Wilson was promoted to full colonel, and Major Nelson and I were promoted to lieutenant colonel. It was the surprise of my life, for I had not reached my twenty-sixth birthday yet. Colonel Wilson was so elated that he ordered free beer for everyone that evening. The troops apparently set out to get even with him for all the pressure he'd put on everyone, for his bar bill the next morning was over $5,000, about four month's pay for a colonel. He was a little piqued the next day but quietly licked his wounds and carried on.

16

D-Day and the Fall Campaign

During D-Day, and for several weeks thereafter, we concentrated on support of the Allied invasion armies. Each time they ran into any truly organized resistance, we'd rain fragmentation and high-explosive bombs down on the enemy. Most of the time, our armies would then immediately march right through them.

On one occasion, on September 17, 1944, the 82nd and the 101st Airborne Divisions were going to drop on Holland near Eindhoven and Nijmegen (Operation "Market Garden"). We preceded them at fifteen thousand feet, trying to eliminate any German defenses in the drop areas with fragmentation bombs set to explode at about fifty feet above the ground. The weather was perfect, and we covered the drop area completely. From my air commander's seat the drop areas looked as if they had been plowed after our drop, and I could not imagine that any life could have withstood that pounding.

By prearrangement, we were briefed to circle along the coast and watch as the C-47s dropped the paratroopers and towed in their gliders. I could not believe what I saw. The German defenses came out of the ground and decimated our troops. Gliders were wrecked everywhere, and our poor paratroopers had to fight for their lives.

The only positive thing I saw that afternoon was Gen. Jimmy Doolittle flying around alone in a P-47, viewing the disaster. It was one of the few times I saw a general officer actually up where the fighting was taking place and exposed to enemy fire. Jimmy Doolittle was a leader.

With our new group commander, Colonel Wilson, came a new set of squadron commanders. Maj. Albert Cox, a tall, quiet gentleman, became commanding officer of the 325th Squadron. Al was from North Carolina via Washington, D.C., where his father had been the Adjutant General of the District of Columbia. He was senior to most of his contemporaries, having been commissioned in ROTC in the late 1930s. More mature than most, he was respected by all who knew him.

The 326th Bomb Squadron's new commander was Capt. Ernest C. "Moose" Hardin, of Louisville, Kentucky. Moose had arrived from flight training in the fall of 1943 and had worked his way up through squadron operations to commander. He was personable and very popular with the troops. Everyone liked him, and he became one of the most respected officers on the base.

The 407th Bomb Squadron gained Maj. William H. Nelson as its new commander. Major Nelson was also an older and more senior officer, who had been the squadron operations officer before being promoted to commander. Four months later he was named group air executive officer, replacing Lt. Col. Rip Riordan.

As Colonel Wilson worked to put a new face on the base, innovation became the watchword. The mess halls were redecorated, and commanders were ordered to eat with the enlisted men at least three meals each week. Buildings were painted, and the new name for the group, "Fame's Favored Few," was surely apt. It stuck like glue. With our new name we settled in for a long, cold winter.

Our troops had liberated Paris in August, and everyone

wanted to visit the city and enjoy its sights and entertainment. We in England had been ordered not to go to the Continent unless on orders for official business, because of the shortage of food, the strain on transportation, etc.

One morning in October, Moose Hardin and I asked Colonel Wilson for a B-17 for a flight to London. Of course he knew we weren't flying to London. One took the train to London, not an airplane. He gave us his consent with a sly smile, and off we went with a crew of seventeen of our friends for our first visit to Paris.

I flew the airplane on the trip over. The weather wasn't too good, but we made it to Le Bourget Airport without mishap and were circling the field in and out of clouds and in low visibility about fifteen hundred feet above the ground. Suddenly the navigator called me and said, "Don't move just yet, but there's an airplane right above us." I looked up right into the belly of C-54 going our same direction. It was almost as if I were flying formation with him. I slid out to the right, fell in behind him, and followed him around the pattern and onto the final approach for the landing runway.

After our landing, a truck met us and began transporting my passengers to the terminal. I remained and helped the flight engineer tie down our airplane and secure the contents, so we were the last ones to get to the terminal. After I'd closed my flight plan, I got on the city bus, which by then was fully loaded with just one seat left, beside an American businessman in civilian clothes. I sat down and introduced myself, and he told me he'd just flown in from the States. He was with the Singer Sewing Machine Company and anxious to get its manufacturing plant in Paris back into production. He pulled a bottle of bourbon from inside his coat and said, "You know, I've got to have a drink. Some damned fool almost flew into us up there over the airport, and I'm shook." I said, "Well sir, you'd better give me one too, for I'm the fellow that almost ran into you."

Paris was wonderful. We found lodging in a small hotel and

began enjoying the sights and clubs. We ended up the second night at the Lido, and the show there was the greatest we'd ever seen. Moose and I were buying drinks for all our crew and a dozen or more ladies of the evening who soon joined us.

We were also joined by a captain and a lieutenant who were P-47 fighter pilots. The lieutenant was so drunk that he kept falling off his chair. Shortly he had disappeared, and I stepped into the men's room and found him passed out on the floor. I was a little disgusted, and back at his table I told the captain what had happened and suggested that he take the lieutenant home. He said, "Sir, don't be too hard on that boy, for he has only been here three weeks and he's been shot down twice already." I said, "If that's the case, go get him and I'll buy him another drink."

The Lido ran the show as long as we'd buy drinks. We closed the place the next morning, with each of us owing about $800, almost a month's pay. It seemed like we'd bought drinks for every whore in Paris.

Our visit to Paris began to present some real problems. There was no food available. The restaurants had almost nothing, and we could not get into an Army mess without orders. I paid a clerk in our hotel ten English pounds, about $40, for half a loaf of bread. Finally, after the third day, we flew home on empty stomachs.

As fall began to fade into winter, our Allied invasion armies had pushed the German army from Holland almost back to the Siegfried line. Our 40th Combat Wing was assigned to support General Patton's 3rd Army. Our support during Patton's battle to capture Aachen, Gelsenkirchen, and Metz was such that we earned three commendations from General Doolittle.

A few weeks earlier, on September 10, we attacked an airplane engine factory at Sindelfingen, Germany. The group ran into heavy and accurate flak while leaving the target and en route home. Lt. Horace Spencer's airplane was badly shot-up and on fire when he gave the order to bail out. S/Sgt. Jack Spratt, a gunner on Spencer's airplane, wrote the following story of this experience:

"I'm writing this on September 15, 1944, so it can be used for further reference or just to jog my memory in future years.

"The day started out with it's usual wake-up call for breakfast, briefing for the mission, parachute checkout, escape kits, equipment for gun positions, cold-weather clothing for high altitude, and transportation to the aircraft. This was normal routine for an experienced crew with ten missions, good ones and some real bad ones. After arriving at the aircraft's hardstand, we all preflight our positions, pulled the props through on the four engines. This prepared us for our takeoff on a journey flight I'll never forget.

"The crew members on this mission were as follows: 1st Lt. Horace L. Spencer, pilot; 2nd Lt. Paul K. Bupp, copilot; 2nd Lt. J. Ableman, navigator; 2nd Lt. Harry J. Cross, Jr., bombardier; S/Sgt. Thomas F. Jenkins, engineer; S/Sgt. John L. Houck, radio operator; S/Sgt. Jack Spratt, ball turret gunner; and Sgt. Leslie G. Spillman, tail gunner. We were all known as "Spence's crew" in the States, and it became our motto in the 92nd Bombardment Group, 326th Bomb Squadron, located at Podington, England, Station #109.

"The takeoff was without any problems, even with the usual early morning fog and mist. We assembled on the English countryside at an altitude high enough for clear skies and sunshine. We joined the other groups and crossed the English Channel on our route to the target.

"Our first problem occurred over the channel with an oil leak on the number three engine. The pilot, Lieutenant Spencer, was able to cope with it and eventually had to feather it. Of course, this left us with one less engine to fly with on this mission. The decision was made by the pilot and the flight engineer, Thomas F. Jenkins, to proceed on the mission. This was no great problem, as we had previously lost three engines on another mission and had to fly at low level back to England, at the end of which Lieutenant Spencer landed the plane with only the number one engine. Therefore, no one on the crew wanted to abort the mission.

"The route to the target was filled with heavy flak. Any place you looked the big 88mm projectiles were bursting, and flak was all around us. When we reached the Initial Point, heavy flak was dense, and we received a direct hit to our number four engine. This made it impossible to maintain our position in the formation, because the plane was losing altitude fast. The aircraft was hit by many bursts of flak, damaging the plane to the point it was almost impossible to fly. The order was given for a standby bail-out.

"We lightened the load by throwing out anything that had weight, such as ammunition and guns. That would make the aircraft keep flying longer. We tried really hard to drop the ball turret from the aircraft, but it was all in vain, as the wrench was not in its place for us to loosen the nuts and bolts. It must have been lost in the battle. We worked with a gun barrel trying to pry it out of the ring gear, without success. By making the plane lighter, our pilot was able to get us closer to friendly lines. A target was located on the ground, a large warehouse, and bombardier Lt. Harry J. McCrossen scored a direct hit, sending a lot of black smoke high into the sky.

"We were informed by S/Sgt. John Houck, our radio operator, that as soon as the plane had gone as far as the pilot could fly it, we would abandon the proud B-17 Flying Fortress, 'Homesick Angel.' The bail-out word came at about eight hundred feet from the ground. We had begun to draw a lot of small-arms fire from rifles, machine guns, 20mm canons, and whatever the Germans could throw up at us. The number two engine was burning, and numbers three and four were damaged beyond repair. That left only the number one engine operating at about half power and us losing altitude very fast. Lieutenant Ableman, the navigator, came back into the waist section and pulled the handle on the waist door, which was the signal for bailing out. S/Sgt. Jenkins followed Ableman out, with Sgt. Hensley, Sgt. Spillman, and I, S/Sgt. Spratt, leaving the plane at about six hundred feet. S/Sgt. Houck was the last man out of the waist section of the plane. Lieutenant Spencer, 2nd Lt. Bupp, and 2nd Lt. McCrossen left the plane from the nose hatch door.

"As I left the waist hatch door, I pushed myself clear of the aircraft tail assembly. This was done so that when the parachute opened it would not hang up on the plane anywhere. Bailing out at high altitude, you were taught or told to freefall for many thousands of feet before pulling the ripcord. But at low altitude it was a different set of rules. I glanced to see if I was clear, being so close to the ground, and pulled the ripcord handle on the chest parachute. The pilot chute came out and filled itself with air. But to my surprise nothing else came out of the chest parachute pack. I said to myself, don't panic, and I began to pull the silk from the parachute pack. I could see it wasn't going to unfold, as some of the layers of the fanfolds were stuck together. I began to separate the folds, which had been stuck together by a burst of flak. The reason for its being hit by flak must have been that the parachute was hanging on the hooks near the ball turret. There was just enough room for me in the ball turret, nothing else. As I was pulling the folds apart, the ground was getting closer and closer. It is only a matter of seconds or minutes from the time you jump at low altitude to landing on the ground. I think I passed everyone on the way down, but it might have been my imagination.

"Your mind takes you back into time. Things flash before your eyes that happened many years ago. Good things and bad things, a time to get right with the Lord. You pray for help according to His will. The most impressive thought came as I remembered the Twenty-third Psalm. To my surprise, during all this small amount of time I was able to get enough of the sealed folds of the parachute apart and, with the help of the little pilot chute, make the big parachute float toward a grove of large trees. I was most grateful that God's handiwork had someone put those trees in that very spot for me to land in, instead of the ground area not more than thirty to fifty feet from the trees. I came down into the trees with a crash and a force that propelled me back upward. When the parachute and harness reached its limits I was like a yo-yo for a few minutes. When all the movement stopped I was about five to ten feet from the ground. Several of the crew members who landed near my position helped me get out of my chute harness, as my weight prevented me from unbuckling the lower clips on the harness.

"The nine crew members were taken to the French home of a Mr. and Mrs. Drauin, where we received some food and drinks. These people treated us so nice and let us stay there until help arrived. The 3rd Army representatives arrived at the French home to pick us up and take the crew to General Patton's 3rd Army Headquarters, just outside of Metz. The General summoned the crew to his command trailer area. To see a gentleman as tall as Patton, a big-boned, stocky man, come down off those steps toward us was quite a sensation for me as well as for the other crew members. What does a staff sergeant, or a lieutenant, say to a man like this? Illustrative of Army aviators, we had paid less attention to military formalities than our infantry counterparts. I wondered, do we come to attention, salute, or what?

"General Patton told us to stand at ease and commended us on our act of bombing the German warehouse despite the battle damage to our plane. There was an awkward few minutes when no one knew what to say. I finally broke the silence by saying, 'Sir, will you sign our short snorter bills?' This broke the silence with laughter, and the general signed our bills. Once we started talking with him, he became just like an old country gentleman, a grandfatherly type you could easily converse with. The General did not look like his pictures, nor did he act like his reputation, 'Old Blood and Guts.' He was glad to meet us because of the air support we were giving the 3rd Army. Each crew member gave him some of our maps from our escape kits. He was most appreciative to have these maps.

"He chatted with us, asking where we were from and other generally expected questions. But unexpectedly the General turned to his aide, Colonel Murray, and said, 'Get me nine Bronze Stars.' I remember the aide explaining to him that couldn't be done because the Bronze Star medal is for ground personnel, not to mention that the aircrew was not under his command. General Patton said again, 'Get me nine Bronze Stars.' Colonel Murray went and got nine Bronze Star medal ribbons. The General pinned a ribbon on each crew member. He also had the Signal Corps photographer take a group picture of the crew with him, and he signed each picture and sent one to each crew member.

"The General then asked Lt. Horace L. Spencer, our pilot, how we would get back to our home base in England. Before Lieutenant Spencer could answer, General Patton said, 'I will provide the transportation back to England in my private C-47.' Patton's C-47 was a Cadillac of a plane compared to what we were used to flying our missions in. The host had a case each of cognac and champagne loaded on the plane for us to take back to our base.

"When we approached for the landing at our base in Podington, England, the pilot of Patton's plane gave his call sign, and the tower recognized it as General Patton's plane. Naturally, they thought Patton was on board, and a number of staff cars came zooming out to meet him. But instead, a group of grungy-looking sergeants and lieutenants came out of the plane. An administrative officer said, 'You're not allowed to wear that Bronze Star Ribbon.' I said, 'Until General Patton tells me not to wear it, I'm going to wear it.'"

When General Patton's C-47 arrived with Lieutenant Spencer and the crew, the pilot delivered a case of cognac and champagne to the group commanders, the group executive officer, and to me as group operations officer. It was an ironic gesture. Here was the Army general who would not let me in his officers' mess in Casablanca now sending me a case of champagne and his autographed picture with Lieutenant Spencer's crew. My, how things did change in two years. I probably should have told General Spaatz of his grand gesture.

17

Aerial Operations

Many spectacular incidents occurred during combat missions. Some were tragic, a few amusing, and all action-packed. Most tragic were those airplanes that took direct hits from flak shells and blew apart in midair. As mentioned earlier, bomber crew members did not wear their parachutes during actual combat, except when alerted to prepare to abandon ship. Instead they wore their chute harnesses and stowed the actual parachute bundles nearby. When the airplane would get a direct hit and blow apart in mid-air, the crewmen would not have the chance to grab the chute. The concussion would blow the parachute apart and, with no weight on the chute, it would flutter through the sky like a leaf in an autumn breeze, while all the bodies, guns, and engines fell like rain earthward.

On one mission I was directed to lead a twelve-ship flight about ten minutes ahead of the bomber train. My mission was to precede the main force to a point upwind of the target and to fill the sky with chaff to foul the antiaircraft radar-aiming equipment. Chaff consisted of thousands of bundles of aluminum foil, cut in strips about a quarter-inch wide and fifteen inches long. When cast out into the slipstream, the bundles would break apart and flutter through the air in great patches. To the radar-aiming devices they looked like airplanes and always drew lots of fire.

On this particular mission the target was Frankfurt. All went as briefed, and I departed the English coast on time, with what I thought was the entire 8th Air Force right behind me. As I proceeded to the target the weather worsened, and visibility was greatly reduced. About the time I arrived over my drop area my radio operator called me to tell me he had just received a mission recall signal. We proceeded to scatter our chaff, and as we turned westward I called our division air commander and asked his position. He answered that the entire bomber train had turned back.

For my little twelve-ship formation it was a chilly feeling. We were out there all alone, forty or fifty miles behind the big formations and just plain sitting ducks. I elected shortly to climb from twenty-six thousand to twenty-nine thousand feet in order to pick up a little speed, also knowing that the German fighters couldn't do much above thirty thousand feet. We made it home without mishap.

While leading another mission in late 1944 we were over Holland and everything seemed to be going too well. The visibility was good, no German flak guns were firing at us, and our 8th Air Force had reduced the German fighter force to the point that it was of little worry to us. Suddenly, I saw on the far horizon some tiny specs maneuvering in such a manner that at times they were almost invisible, then suddenly very easy to see—somewhat like a group of starlings flying around a meadow, or the sensation produced when opening a venetian blind. Several crew members also saw this phenomenon, and we were conjecturing on what it might be when, as we drew closer, the tiny specks rose up in the sky behind one tiny speck. It was about forty American fighters, all chasing a lone German Me-109. They were hot after him as he climbed skyward, then suddenly rolled over and headed straight for our formation. It was his only chance to escape, and he had to take it. As he approached in his dive for our lead ship, every .50-caliber machine gun on every B-17 in formation began firing at him, leaving a cone of tracer bullets that looked like a funnel right on his nose—and of course right into the American fighters that were chasing him. The German fighter passed right through the middle of our formation as the American fighters peeled off in all directions. My ball turret gunner reported that he disappeared into the clouds below with no apparent damage.

Again, leading a mission across the Zuider Zee one morning, someone called out a B-17 at 12 o'clock high. I looked up and watched a B-17 diving straight down at a terrific speed. The entire tail section had been blown off, apparently from direct flak hit, and the plane fell into a power dive. At about eight thousand feet, the right wing broke off and the remaining fuselage fell in a ball of fire. A few seconds later we saw the tail section, consisting of the rudder and both horizontal stabilizers, fluttering back and forth like a leaf in the breeze. A few days later, *Stars and Stripes*, the U.S. Army newspaper, reported that two gunners rode that B-17 tail to the ground without injury!

In yet another raid, I was leading my group into Germany at twenty-six thousand feet. The visibility below was poor, but I could see some B-24 formations at about twenty to twenty-one thousand feet. Two of these B-24 squadrons were flying beside one another, separated by heavy contrails produced by the preceding formations. The two squadrons were flying on a converging course but unable to see each other. As they drew closer I began calling every call sign that I could think of in an effort to warn them. They finally flew into each other and disappeared into the heavy part of the contrails.

December 1944 was again a very busy month for us. We were briefing and flying missions almost every day, dispatching an average of nearly five hundred bombers per month with very few losses. It was a different and much easier war for us now. The German Luftwaffe was nearly wiped out, and we now owned all of France, Belgium, and Holland. Unless you were so unfortunate as to take a direct flak hit, you could nearly always make it back to friendly lines and bail out if necessary.

In mid-December, Wehrmacht General von Runstedt began his push through the Ardennes toward Antwerp that resulted in the famous Battle of the Bulge. He selected a time when he knew the weather would not permit our Air Force to operate. We prepared and briefed almost the same missions every day from December 16 to December 23, without being able to launch. Finally the weather cleared and we could get airborne. Our ground troops were desperate, and we felt a great urgency to go help them. It was also my turn to be the air commander. Our target was a road and rail intersection behind the German lines. We were out to destroy their transportation facilities and cut off their supplies. It was to be a simple mission for us, and I felt so confident that I wore an electrically heated suit for the first time. They were much like an electric blanket, with a rheostat, and were very comfortable in the subzero temperatures at high altitude. The only problem was that if you had to bail out, you lost your electrical system and were sure to be awfully cold. And if you survived bail out, you might have to spend the rest of the war in a prisoner-of-war camp in that funny-looking suit. Hence, few people wore them.

We got our airplanes off and our formation formed up without a problem, and as we left the English coast everything seemed to be fine. I had been up every night for a week and was worn out, so I called the navigator and told him I was going to take a nap and to call me before we got to the Initial Point to begin our bomb run.

I was dozing off when all of a sudden the airplane was hit with a loud thud. It began to rock back and forth, and shrapnel began to rattle along the skin of the airplane. I awoke with a start and asked who was shooting at us. The bombardier answered that tanks were firing at us! I looked down through the snow-covered forest and, sure enough, I could see what looked like tanks firing at us. The Germans had advanced forty miles beyond the lines we'd been briefed on!

The remainder of our mission went as planned. We hit our targets, the marshalling yards at Erlangen, Germany, with all thirty-seven airplanes and with excellent bombing results. Gen. Howard M. Turner, our 40th Combat Wing commander, gave us a special commendation as follows: "I wish to extend to you and all officers and men of the bombardment groups which participated in the mission of 23 December, 1944, my congratulations for the excellent maneuver in which the mission was executed. Operating in extremely adverse weather conditions, these units exhibited a high degree of determination and skill in attacking the marshalling yards at Erlangen, Germany, and landing in adverse weather conditions without loss of a single aircraft. Excellent bombing results were obtained. Convey to participating officers and men my appreciation of a job well done."

After we had returned to our home base and parked our airplane, I started to climb out of my seat when I heard a clunk-clunk sound beneath me. I turned, and there in my seat was a large piece of shrapnel; it had come through the side of the airplane and through my metal seat right into my rear! It apparently was spent as it entered my seat for it did not injure me in any way. I had flown about forty missions all over the Continent by this time without being hit, and here, on what I would call a milk run, I'd nearly bought the farm. I kept that piece of shrapnel as a souvenir of the war and used it as a paperweight until someone stole it and a B-17 clock off of my desk.

The following morning was Christmas Eve, 1944. My friend Pam Humphrey Firman again invited Maj. Jim Smyrl and me to Standbridge Earles for Christmas. Jim arranged for one of his squadron crews to fly us to an airfield near Ramsey en route to the rest house.

When we arrived, the field was full of C-47s being loaded with the newly arrived 17th Airborne Division. They had just come from the States and were on their way to a new forward base near Romilly sur Seine. I inquired about my college friend, Bill Miller, and found him in the chaplain's office, scared to death. They were all set for the entire division to parachute into their new base, and he thought it would be into a concentration of the

German army. We relieved him somewhat when we explained that the front lines were well east of his new base.

Stanbridge Earles was a wonderful place for Christmas, and Pam Firman told us that Lady Mountbatten had invited us to her nearby farm for Christmas dinner. Lord Louis Mountbatten was, of course, in India running the show for the British, and his good lady was entertaining the troops back home. Jim and I were accompanied by two U.S. Army officers and a U.S. Navy lieutenant. The Navy lieutenant was filled with self-importance and talked almost constantly. He made it clear that he felt the Navy was the superior service, and only through its leadership were we winning the war.

Lady Mountbatten was a very gracious hostess, and she asked each of us where we were from. The lieutenant let her know immediately that Boston was his home and how Boston was the centerpiece of American civilization. When she got to me I explained that my home was Charleston, West Virginia. She quickly said, "Oh, I have a great friend from Bluefield. Do you know where it is?" I said, "Of course, my number one girlfriend [my bride] lives there." She replied that her friend Mary Lee Fairbanks, wife of Douglas Fairbanks Jr., was from Bluefield, West Virginia, and that she had once gone with her to visit Mary's mother in Bluefield. I told her that my Bluefield lady's parents were close friends of Dr. and Mrs. Epling, Mary Lee's parents. Then she spent the next ten minutes talking about her friends the Fairbankses and about Bluefield. Boston was never again mentioned. The lieutenant was dumbfounded.

We had a delightful time at the Mountbattens' farm, and my friend Maj. Jim Smyrl was a guest at the Mountbattens' place in London several times thereafter. Departing Stanbridge Earles for the last time, I thanked Pam Firman for all her hospitality and told her I hoped our next meeting would be in Cleveland, Ohio.

18

My War's End

January 1945 was a tough time for everyone at my 92nd Bomb Group. The weather was almost unbearable. Our group had been in England for nearly thirty months, and all of us old-timers were war weary.

As group operations officer, I would often accompany my assistant for airplane maintenance, Maj. Jim Boutty, around our airbase to check on the ground crew's progress in getting airplanes ready to fly for the following day. We were flying missions nearly two out of every three days now, and many planes were shot full of holes and had other damage that took time to repair. We had no hangars for daily maintenance, so most of these repairs had to be done outside in the snow and cold rain, at night with poor lighting. This experience made me really feel for the poor mechanics.

Along with the worst weather in the three winters that we had been there, we were also encountering ever-increasing operational activity. We received combat orders almost every evening. We briefed our air crews seventeen times and flew thirteen missions, twice as many as in January 1944, and for each mission we put up thirty to forty B-17s, again almost twice as many as a year before. All of this in ice and snow and in the coldest days of the war.

Most of this increased air activity was due to the plight of our Army ground forces trying to force open the Siegfried Line—in probably the worst conditions of the ground war (so aptly described in Stephen Ambrose's book *Citizen Soldiers*). Several of our air crewmen who had crashed or bailed out near the front lines came back with stories of the pitiful plight of the ground combat troops.

February was in many aspects more difficult than most months. We briefed our air crews twenty-four times and flew sixteen missions, putting up nearly six hundred B-17s and losing only four, a record for our group.

I led our group and the 1st Air Division on an attack of the oil refinery at Lutzkendorf on February 7. Cloud conditions covered the target, and we bombed Saalfeld as a secondary target. On February 9, I again led our group back to Lutzkendorf. This time the weather was clear, and we hit our target with excellent results. The refinery was totally destroyed.

Though the antiaircraft fire was heavy and accurate and several of our aircraft received heavy damage, every plane made it back to base and only one crewman was killed, T/Sgt. George Cooke of the 325th Squadron. More than fifty combat crewmen finished their combat tours on this mission, the most in the history of our group.

It also ended my second combat tour. I had flown forty combat missions. For the past six months, my office had worked all night on an average of two out of three days. In many instances we would brief twice in one day when we were sending formations to different targets. This routine had worn me down physically to the point that I was becoming short with my peers and assistants, and I had begun to realize it was time to take a break. We all realized also that the war was coming to an end, for our forces and the Russians had the Germans in an ever-tightening box. It was only a matter of time now.

I had been in England for more than thirty-one months. I asked Col. Jim Wilson, my group commander, to let me transfer back to the States. He agreed and assigned Maj. John McKee as my assistant and my replacement upon my departure. In late February I received orders reassigning me to Stateside duty and ordering me to report to the personnel center in Liverpool for the trip home.

After a much-needed thirty-day leave at home, my bride and I reported to the Army Air Corps Officer Replacement Center in Miami Beach. It was now April and a good time to be in Florida. A lot of my old friends were there, and we had great times awaiting reassignment.

Slowly the lieutenants, captains, and even the majors found assignments, but no one wanted another flying lieutenant colonel. All of the commanders of the Stateside bases had senior staff officers that had been with them throughout the war. They all knew their jobs well and in many instances had become good friends with their commanders. No one wanted a senior lieutenant colonel arriving and outranking the officers who'd been there a long time. Hence, I along with a few others spent several extra weeks in Miami Beach. One of my friends there was Col. Butch Helton, who'd been a group commander in the South Pacific. No one wanted him either, and he suggested one day that we'd still be in Miami when the Japs surrendered.

I was really enjoying Miami Beach, until I got a notice to report to the administrative office. I was sure this meant a reassignment, so I arrived on time loaded with curiosity. One of the finance officers pulled out my file and began to question me about when I'd joined the service, when I'd been commissioned, and the dates of my promotions to first lieutenant, captain, major, and lieutenant colonel.

After running a few figures through his calculator he turned to me and asked if I'd ever filed an income tax. I replied that I had not, as I had been overseas since three months after flying school. He then ran a few more figures through his calculator and turned to me and said, "You owe $3,800 in income taxes, and you have thirty days to pay up."

I was stunned. I wasn't even certain that I had that much cash on hand and, besides, I wasn't sure that an income tax was applicable to me. He made me sign a statement acknowledging the fact that I owed the money, gave me a copy of it and a completed income tax return with envelope, and bid me goodbye. He ruined my whole day.

About two weeks later, my old friend Col. William "Darky" Reid called me. He was now the deputy commander of the 3rd Army Air Force at Drew Field in Tampa, Florida. He explained to me that he could get me assigned to any of his bases, but with my date of rank I'd get a better job if I would agree to go to Avon Park Army Air Field, located just south of Orlando.

I took his suggestion and finally found myself en route to Avon Park in early June 1945. My reception there was so bad that it was almost comical. I felt like the so-called "bastard at the family reunion." The base commander was an old-timer (maybe World War I) who wasn't current in any type of airplane on his field. The director of training was a former Civil Aviation Administration employee who'd been at Avon Park since it had opened. They had been training B-17 crews throughout the whole war, and a combat returnee with a chest full of ribbons was the last thing they wanted to see.

I was given an assignment as the director of training operations, which consisted of scheduling training missions and cross-country navigational flights to Havana, Puerto Rico, etc.

In early July, Colonel Reid called me to come to a meeting at 3rd Air Force Headquarters. There he placed me on temporary duty to command a combat demonstration team, consisting of squadrons of P-51s, P-47s, B-25s, B-26s, A-20s, B-17s, and nine C-47s (to carry our mechanics, tools, and spare parts).

We put on air shows at Detroit and a few other places and then were ordered to Deming Army Airfield, in southern New

Mexico. We were told that we were to put on a bombing and strafing demonstration for a group of congressmen and other government officials. A mock airport, complete with wooden airplanes, was our target—all in view of open bleacher seating on a nearby hillside. We were given one day to practice our show. We scheduled the B-17s in first, at about three thousand feet above the target terrain, followed by the B-25s and B-26s. Then last came the P-47s and the P-51s to strafe the place clean.

All went well until we neared the target. No one told us that there would be antiaircraft fire—using blanks. All of my crews had just returned from combat, and when the flak suddenly burst all around us, my formation broke apart and the airplanes took off in all directions!

The next day, at the real show, we all understood that we were not actually being shot at, and the show went on almost perfectly. After our demonstration, all my crews and maintenance people wanted to go to El Paso and cross the border to Jaurez, Mexico. Since we had no return time scheduled, I agreed, and we unloaded our C-47s and flew everyone who wanted to go to Biggs Field and got transportation to Juarez. We were all enjoying the evening when suddenly someone came running into our restaurant, yelling that the sky was on fire. We all went outside to view the huge light in the heavens to the north of us. No one could figure out what had happened. It was three weeks later that we learned that we'd witnessed the test explosion of the first atomic bomb in history.

I arrived back at Avon Park to learn that the base had been ordered closed. We began immediately to transfer to storage our B-17s. Air Transport Command pilots were sent to fly away our airplanes.

One morning I happened to note on the schedule the impending arrival of one Capt. Russell Kerr with crew, assigned to fly out one of our B-17s. I knew it had to be my first instructor in primary flying school, back in Canton, Mississippi, who had washed all of his students out and had given me such a hard time. I couldn't wait to see him now almost four years later, I as a lieutenant colonel and he as a captain.

I had the control tower notify me when he landed, and I took a position that blocked the door through which he had to pass to get into base operations. As he approached the doorway I stood firm, looking him straight in the eyes. When he could move no farther he looked at me and said, "Pardon me, sir, may I come in?" I looked at him and replied, "Not until you come to attention and render the usual military greeting, Captain Kerr." He looked puzzled, then a faint smile came across his face, and he saluted. I returned the salute and said, "Kerr, I just wanted you to never forget me and my friends that you washed out of flying school, and also, don't ever approach me again without saluting. Do you understand?" He meekly replied, "Yes, sir," and I laughed and walked away.

By early September I was transferred to the Gulfport Army Air Field, Mississippi. Upon arrival I was assigned to the B-29 school and spent the next month learning to fly the B-29. While it was the best of our bombers, it was a dog to fly: heavy, cumbersome, underpowered, and slow. It was not a fun airplane.

Shortly thereafter came orders to close the base. Our officers and men were leaving the service in droves. Soon we didn't have enough maintenance men to keep our B-29s flyable. Those that could fly were flown to the airplane boneyard in Tucson, Arizona. The rest were cut up and loaded onto rail cars and sent to junkyards. We then had to travel to Keesler Army Airfield to do our required flying.

By the summer of 1946, even though I'd been given a commission in the Regular Army Air Corps, I began to wonder whether it was the life I wanted. As a lieutenant colonel on flying status, I was being paid nearly $1,200 per month, a huge sum for a twenty-six–year-old and more than double the salary of my father, who had been agriculture commissioner of West Virginia for fourteen years. I'd also been offered jobs with American and Pan American Airlines, but I couldn't foresee being very happy in later years flying an airplane every day from Chicago to Los Angeles. It seemed to me there had to be more to life than flying airplanes every day.

It had been a great four years, the most exciting of my life. Being a part of a combat unit, fighting for the high ideals of freedom for the world, was above all a very satisfying adventure and a positive accomplishment, whereas peacetime service offered little. I felt the time had come to go home and go to work. My good wife agreed. In June 1946 we said goodbye to our Gulfport friends and headed for the hills of West Virginia.

19

A Look Back

Hindsight, always being twenty-twenty, makes it easy to look back and find our flaws and mistakes. But when one looks at the circumstances under which we went to war, criticism is probably not the order of the day.

As late as 1938 the entire Army Air Corps had fewer than fifty thousand total officers. Only a few had flown the B-18, the biggest bomber of the Air Corps at that time. It was little more than a bomber conversion of another new airplane, the DC-3. Only a few pilots had flown the early versions of the B-17 and the B-24, and most of those men were Wright Field test pilots. By 1941 only a very few senior Air Corps officers were permitted to fly the B-17. It wasn't until late 1941 that we had one so-called combat-ready strategic B-17 group outside the United States—the 19th Bomb Group, which had been sent to the Pacific. The demands of assembling a combat-capable 8th Air Force and sending it over fortified Europe seem staggering in retrospect.

No pilot in any Air Corps bomber or fighter group had ever participated in or observed an air force at war. Of the original pilots of the 8th Air Force in 1942, none had received any formal training in instrument flying, and neither England nor Africa had any instrument-landing aids in place throughout the entire war.

We probably should have given night bombing a try, for with our higher altitude capability and superior firepower we might have had fewer losses than the RAF. We certainly would have had fewer losses than we incurred with precision daylight bombing.

Our defeat of the Luftwaffe (Operation Pointblank) was undoubtedly one of our greatest contributions to America's crusade in Europe, for there is great doubt as to the degree of success our ground forces could have had in the invasion and drive across western Europe if the German air forces could have freely attacked them. In addition, our carpet bombing ahead of our attacking armies made Allied efforts much more successful, and our fighter sweeps of the enemy's ground transportation and troops kept the Germans on the defensive night and day.

I would be remiss if I failed to address the superior combat leadership of the group and squadron commanders in the 8th and 9th Army Air Forces. They were the key element in all of the successes of the air attacks on Europe in World War II. There were many instances when one could have justified a mission's turning back against overwhelming odds, but I cannot recall a single such occurrence. To be sure, there were many instances when individual airplanes turned back, many from engine failure, many more from fear. But the squadrons and groups pressed on.

Finally, I'd like to mention an element of our air combat forces that stands out in my mind and makes World War II different from all of the wars that followed. I refer to what I call attitude and ingenuity. World War II was not a political war in the same sense as the Korean and Vietnam conflicts. The greater part of our leadership was in the field, and everyone was doing all that he could to defeat the Axis powers. Not one of the leaders I served was acting first to protect his rank or pension or to curry the favor of commanding generals. The job came first, and if we couldn't get to the briefed target we would pick out another one—a factory, rail yard, or storage dump—and we'd attack it. If Hanoi had been a city in Germany in World War II, it would have been attacked regularly. In the Vietnam conflict, attacking the enemy's capital and certain other targets would have been cause for a general court martial.

The 8th Air Force of World War II was probably the most effective fighting force this nation has produced. The valiant men who went ashore on D-Day and fought the German armies in 1944 and 1945 will attest to this fact.

Afterword

Three months after arriving home, the adjutant general of the State of West Virginia asked me to accept the position of commander of the state's first Air National Guard Squadron. It seemed like the right thing to do, and I accepted the challenge of building a new reserve fighter squadron. Forty-eight months later I found myself leading this squadron back on active duty in the Air Force in the Korean War.

Following service in the Korean War, I received promotion to full colonel and, in 1962, was appointed assistant adjutant general, with a promotion to brigadier general. I continued my service as a weekend Air National Guard officer until my retirement in 1977.

Appendix

Statistics of the Fame's Favored Few, from the *Official History of the 92nd Bombardment Group*

Creation

August 1942: Assigned to the 8th Air Force

Wing and Command Assignments

August 1942: 8th Bomber Command, 1st Bombardment Wing

May 1943: 8th Bomber Command, 102nd PC Bombardment Wing

September 13, 1943: 8th Bomber Command, 1st Bombardment Division, 40th Combat Bombardment Wing

January 8, 1944: 1st Bombardment Division, 40th Combat Bombardment Wing

January 1, 1945: 1st Air Division, 40th Combat Bombardment Wing

Squadrons

325th Bombardment Squadron
326th Bombardment Squadron

327th Bombardment Squadron
407th Bombardment Squadron

Stations

Bovingdon: from August 18–28, 1942, to January 4–11, 1943
Alconbury: from January 4–11, 1943, to September 11–15, 1943
Podington: from September 11–15, 1943, to May 20–July 9, 1945

92nd Bomb Group Commanders

Lt. Col. James S. Sutton (March 27, 1942, to May 1, 1943)
Lt. Col. Bascombe R. Lawrence (May 2, 1943, to May 23, 1943)
Lt. Col. William M. Reid (May 23, 1943, to Sept. 27, 1944/Wounded
    in Action, Aug. 26, 1944)
Lt. Col. James W. Wilson (September 27, 1944, to August 4, 1945)

Total Combat Missions

308

Total Credit Sorties

8,633

Total Bomb Tonnage

41,658,000 lbs.

Major Awards

Distinguished Unit Citation (January 11, 1944)
Congressional Medal of Honor to F/O John C. Morgan (July 26,
    1943)

Items of Note

Oldest group in the 8th Air Force

First Bomb Group to make nonstop flight to the United Kingdom (August 1942)

Only unit in 8th Air Force to fly the experimental YB-40 in combat

Created the 8th Bomber Command 1/11th Combat Crew Replacement Center (August 1942 to May 1943)

Flew secret Disney rocket bomb missions (early 1945)

Led the 8th Air Force on its last mission during World War II

Postwar: Absorbed into the 306th Bomb Group, February 28, 1946. Reactivated on August 4, 1946, as a B-29 unit (redesignated as the 448th Bomb Group); flew missions in Korean War. Converted to a B-36 unit in 1951. Later became a B-52 unit as the 92nd Bombardment Wing.

Index

1st Air Division, 58, 83, 86, 93, 101, 124, 163, 165, 167, 188

2nd Air Division, 58, 93, 114

3rd Air Force, 190

3rd Air Division, 54, 58, 83, 85, 94, 101, 114, 168

4th Fighter Group, 49, 59

5th Army, 40

5th U.S. Army Air Corps Service Command, 15

1/11th Combat Crew Replacement Center, 7, 26, 48, 52, 85, 112

12th Tactical Air Force, 30, 150

13th Combat Wing, 93

15th Air Force, 58

17th Airborne Division, 185

19th Bomb Group, 79

40th Combat Wing, 54, 88, 110, 121, 163, 175, 185

56th Fighter Group, 49, 58, 59, 152, 155

91st Bomb Group, 49, 52, 53

93rd Bomb Group, 53

95th Bomb Group, 51, 52, 53, 90, 91, 93

97th Bomb Group, 1, 3, 37, 48, 53

100th Bomb Group, 93

301st Bomb Group, 1, 3, 37, 53

303rd Bomb Group, 53

305th Bomb Group, 53, 54, 55, 67, 68, 88, 110, 121, 121, 169, 170

306th Bomb Group, 53, 54, 55, 67, 68, 88, 110, 121, 169, 170

325th Bomb Squadron, 3, 68, 85, 112, 113, 188

326th Bomb Squadron, 22, 60, 114, 176

327th Bomb Squadron, 4, 60

369th Bomb Squadron, 70

382nd Bomb Group, 55, 124

384th Bomb Group, 88, 152, 163

390th Bomb Group, 93

407th Bomb Squadron, 2, 3, 18, 22

482nd (Pathfinder) Bomb Group, 112, 124. *See also* H2X

Ableman, Lt. J., 176, 177
AFCE, 106
Ahrenholtz, Lt. Augustus C., 60, 111
Air Force Escape and Evasion Society, 149
Air Force Redistribution Center, 154
Air National Guard, 49
Alaskan Command, 8
Alconbury, 48, 51, 52, 56, 85, 99, 112
Alford, David, 27, 124
Algiers, 31, 32, 42
Allied Force Headquarters, 30, 39, 40
Ambrose, Stephen (*Citizen Soldiers*), 188
American Cemetery, Maddingly, England, 25
American Eagle Squadrons, 49, 59
American Red Cross, 110, 148
Anderson, Louis, 38, 41
Army Air Corps Officer Replacement Center, 189
Armstrong, Lt. Gen. Frank, 55, 68
Arnold, Gen. Henry H., 2, 150
Ashendorf, Holland, 65
Asher, Lt., 86
Athenry, Ireland, 46
Atlas Mountains, 35, 37
Austin, Lt. Charles, 2
Avon Park Army Air Base, Fla., 77

Bailey, Constance, 154
Bailey, Capt. Frank, 12
Bangor, Maine, 1, 20, 21, 22
Barnes, Brig. Gen. Gladeon M., 42
Barry, N., 28
Battle of the Bulge, 184

Bedford Key Club, 70
Belongia, Capt. Blair B., 65, 66, 152, 165, 166
Benedict, Capt. John T., 156
Berlin Olympics, 21
Bermuda, 22
Billy Rose's Aquacade, 21
Black Thursday, 97, 100
Blake, Jules, 142, 146, 147
Blanchard, Loren E., 28
Bock, Lt., 126
Bolland, R.C., Flying Sgt., 44
Bomb Groups:
    19th, 79
    91st, 49, 52, 53
    93rd, 53
    95th, 51, 52, 53, 90, 91, 93
    97th, 1, 3, 37, 48, 53
    100th, 93
    301st, 1, 3, 37, 53
    303rd, 53
    305th, 53, 54, 55, 67, 68, 88, 110, 121, 121, 169, 170
    306th, 53, 54, 55, 67, 68, 88, 110, 121, 169, 170
    382nd, 55, 124
    384th, 88, 152, 163
    390th, 93
    482nd (Pathfinder), 112, 124. *See also* H2X
Bomb Squadrons:
    325th, 3, 68, 85, 112, 113, 188
    326th, 22, 60, 114, 176
    327th, 4, 60
    369th, 70
    407th, 2, 3, 18, 22
Boone, Maj. Marshall T., 158, 159, 160
Bos, Mr., 132, 133, 134, 135
Boston, Mass., 3, 20, 186

Boussiere, Monsieur, 73
Bovington, England, 1, 4, 24, 26, 27, 28, 42, 47, 50, 68, 85, 112
Bow, Clara, 49
Boutty, Maj. James, 187
Brietenback, Lou, 149
Briggs, Ruth M., 38
Brousseau, Col. Andre, 98, 164
Browning, Commander, 28
Bruce, Lt. Ralph, 65
Buck, Maj. Willie, 3, 61, 62
Buddenbaum, Lt. Otto, 70
Buenos Aires, Argentina, 32
Bulge, battle of the, 184
Bupp, Lt. Paul K., 176, 177
Burtonwood Air Depot, 27

Campbell, Lt. Robert, 62, 63, 64
Canton, Miss., 9
Casablanca, Morocco, 31, 35, 36, 41, 42
Charleston, W.Va., 2, 51, 77, 161, 186
Chorak, Lt. Francis, 7
Clark, Gen. Mark, 40
Clarksburg, W.Va., 8
Clemson University, 24
Cleveland Diocese, 56
Clough, Lt., 105
College Pilot Training Program, 8
Collins, Lt. Clyde B., 11, 28, 39, 43
Columbus, Miss., 13, 14, 16
Combat Crew Replacement Center, 1/11th, 7, 26, 48, 52, 85, 112
Congleton, James, 16
Congressional Medal of Honor, 24
Cooke, T/Sgt. George, 188
Coolcou, Dr. Jacques, 73
Copenhaver, Lt. Betty, 154

Corbel, Monsieur L'Abbe, 73
Corrie, Robert, 16
Cothren, S/Sgt. Archie, 5, 7, 25
County Galway, Ireland, 24
Cox, Col. Albert, 173
Crane, Col. Joseph T., 10
Cross, Lt. Harry J., 176
Cunningham, Maj. Gen. Joseph, 8
Curtis, Col. Edward, 35, 36

Dace, Lt. William, 162
D-Day, 58, 155, 172
Delval, Eric, 73
Deming Army Air Field, N.Mex., 190
Dempsey, Lt. James, 4, 6, 25
Devers, Gen. Jacob, 42, 44, 46, 150
Dinton, Jeanne-Lou, 72
Dinton, Madame, 72, 73
Doolittle, Lt. Gen. James, 30, 37, 150, 151, 173, 175
Drezmal, Alene, 38
Duckworth, Lt. Col. Joseph, 16
Duff, Lt. D.V., 33, 40, 41
Duke University, 73
Dulag Luft, 76
Dwyer, Maj. John P., 52
Dwyer, Lt. Col. Larry, 152

Eaker, Lt. Gen. Ira C., 7, 25, 45, 47, 48, 52, 64, 150
Eastern Airlines, 16, 57
Eastman Kodak Company, 60
Eaton, F/O Howard F., 165, 166, 167
Eaton, Maj. Gen. Robert, 79, 80, 81
Edris, Lt. Pete, 67
Egan, Capt. Joseph, 49, 152, 154
Eidson, T/Sgt., 102, 103, 105
Eisenhower, Gen. Dwight D., 30, 31, 150

Empire State Building, 20
Erlangen, Germany, 184, 185
European Theater of Operations, 47
Everts, Weinik, 137

1st Air Division, 58, 83, 86, 93, 101, 124, 163, 165, 167, 188
4th Fighter Group, 49, 59
5th Army, 40
5th U.S. Army Air Corps Service Command, 15
15th Air Force, 58
40th Combat Wing, 54, 88, 110, 121, 163, 175, 185
56th Fighter Group, 49, 58, 59, 152, 155
407th Bomb Squadron, 2, 3, 18, 22
482nd (Pathfinder) Bomb Group, 112, 124. *See also* H2X
Fellows, Lt. James, 13
Feldon, Madame, 74
Firman, Pamela Humphrey, 111, 123, 185, 186
Fiske, Maj. Gardiner, 3
Fitzgerald, Capt. Joseph, 152
Foley, S/Sgt. John E., 64, 108
Ford, S/Sgt., James L., 63, 64, 104
Fort Hayes, Ohio, 8
Foster, Capt. James B., 19
Fracchia, Lt. Joseph, 7
Francis, Kay, 26
Frankfurt Am Main, Germany, 76, 124, 182
Fretay, Henri Du, 72

Gale, Adm. H.M., 28, 29
Galway Bay, Ireland, 44
Gander, Newfoundland, 1, 23
Gelsenkirchen, Germany, 113, 167, 175

Geneva Convention, 46
Germany, T/Sgt., 110
Gibralter, 28, 29, 30, 42
Gibson, Capt. "Hoot," 61, 62
Glycine Clinic, 39
Greenland, 1, 2
Greenville, Miss., 12, 14
Griffith, Col. James, 22, 54, 60, 62
Goedkoop, Jan, 135, 136, 137, 142
Gosselink, Mr., 132
Gulf Port Army Air Field, Miss., 192

H2X, 84, 124
Hagerstown, Md., 12
Hampton, Lt. Larry, 31
Hannover, Germany, 61, 65
Hardin, Lt. Gen. Ernest C., 81, 173, 174
Harmon, Maj. James, 99
Harris, Air Marshall Sir Arthur, 59
Helton, Col. Butch, 189
Hermance, Lt. Alan E., 65
Hertfordshire, England, 1
Hodges, Gen. Courtney H., 148
Hogan, Lt. Alec, 51
Hope, Bob, 51
Hormell, Maj. Earl, 42, 43
Hotel Aletti, 32, 33
Hotel Victoria, 31, 32
Houck, S/Sgt. John L., 176, 177
Hughes, Capt. Henry A., 60, 80, 97, 98, 99, 102, 108, 111
Hulings, Capt. Thomas, 22, 27, 28, 36, 43, 44, 45, 47, 49
Huls, Germany, 59

Iceland, 1
Irish Home Guard, 45
Irwin, Lt. Asa J., 63

Jackson, Miss., 9
James, Harry, 22
Jenkins, S/Sgt. Thomas F., 176, 177
Johnson, Capt. Hans, 83
Johnson, Sgt. Robert, 83
Jolson, Al, 26
Jones, Dr. Isaac M., 51

Keck, Lt. Col. Robert, 4, 5, 6, 20, 23, 34, 60, 113, 156
Kelly, Capt. Charles, 13
Kelly, Capt. Colin, 79
Kentucky Military Institute, 161
Kernan, Raphael F., 98, 101
Kerr, Russell, 10, 191
Kiel, Germany, 79
Knaben, Norway, 114
Knowles, Capt. William M., 21, 25
Kontinental Gummiwerke A.G. Waren, Walderstrasse, 62
Koske, Lt. Keith, 62, 64

Lafayette Escadrille, 3
La Fresnay Prison, 74, 76
Lamballe, France, 73
Langford, Francis, 51
Langford Lodge, 47
Lawrence, Lt. Col. Bascombe R., 52, 112
LeBourget Airport, 174
LeMay, Gen. Curtis E., 54, 83, 167, 168
Lennox, Lt. Col. Leslie, 90
Lille, France, 3, 5, 7, 54, 113
Link Instrument Trainer, 18
Littlepage, Lt. Joseph, 161
Littlepage, Kemp, Sr., 161
Locke, Lt. William B., 114, 115, 116, 117, 118, 119
Lorient, France, 70, 74

Luke, Lord, 113
Luper, Capt. James, 9
Lutzkendorf, Germany, 188

MacArthur, Gen. Douglas, 79
MacDill Army Air Field, 1, 17, 18
Mahurin, Col. Walker, 152, 155
Maison Blanche Airport, 31, 39
Marshall, Gen. George C., 161
Maxwell Army Air Field, 9
Mayfair, Mitzi, 26, 51
McBrooks, Maj. Gen. Edward, 42
McClure, T/Sgt. John A., 64
McCrossen, Lt. Harry J., 177
McKee, Maj. John, 189
McLaughlin, Capt. James K., 107
Meaulte, France, 2, 3
Memphis, Tenn., 2, 3
Menjou, Adolph, 51
Merseburg, Germany, 9
Miller, William E., 185
Miller, Lt. Hubert, 24, 165
Milliken, F/O Willard, 49
Mississippi Institute of Aeronautics, 9
Mississippi State College for Women, 15
Mitchell, Gen. "Billy," 58, 59
Mitchell Field, 21
Mooseburg, Germany, 76
Morgan, F/O John, 63, 64
Mountbatten, Lady Edwina C.A., 186
Mountbatten, Lord Louis, 186
Mount Holyoke College, 20
Mustoe, Col. Anthony "Tony," 167

19th Bomb Group, 79
91st Bomb Group, 49, 52, 53
93rd Bomb Group, 53

95th Bomb Group, 51, 52, 53, 90, 91, 93
97th Bomb Group, 1, 3, 37, 48, 53
Nelson, Col. William H., 173
New York City, 20, 21
No Ball targets, 156

100th Bomb Group, 93
Oberkamp, Mr., 128
Oberon, Merle, 26, 51
O'Grady, Capt. Edward T., 60, 97, 102, 106, 107, 108, 109
Olebar family (Hinwick House), 113
Operation Market Garden, 172
Operation Overlord, 30
Operation Torch, 30, 48
Oran, Morocco, 31, 37
Oschersleben, Germany, 119
Ott, Maj. George, 104
Ouijda, Morocco, 40

Parker, Capt. Donald, 54, 63
Parks Aviation Corporation, 9
Pathe News, 50
Pathfinder Group (482nd Bomb Group), 112, 124. *See also* H2X
Patton, Gen. George S., 35, 36, 37, 76, 147, 157, 175, 176, 179, 180
Peabody Hotel, 12
Pearl Harbor, 11, 12, 41, 57, 79
Peaslee, Col. Budd, 57, 88, 101, 102, 103, 104, 105, 107, 109, 162
Piccadilly Circus, 25
Pinette, Mattie (WAC officer), 38
Pittsburgh, Pa., 10
Plain Dealing, La., 13
Podington, England, 99, 112, 119, 135, 160, 180

Ponte, S/Sgt. Eugene F., 64
Port Wreath, England, 27, 28
Prestwick, Scotland, 2, 24

QDM, 43

Radio City Music Hall, 21
Randolph Field, Texas, 10
Rankin, Capt. William Q., 14, 15
Reecher, Kenneth, 12, 17
Reed, Capt. Robert, 54
Reedy, Capt. Jack, 31
Regensburg, Germany, 38
Reid, Col. William M., 18, 53, 57, 58, 79, 109, 112, 113, 123, 124, 152, 158, 163, 165, 166, 167, 169, 190
Reishman, Vincent, 56
Rennes, France, 70
Republic Aviation Corporation, 155
Riordan, Lt. Col. "Rip," 68, 170, 173
Rockettes, 21
Rogers, Martha (WAC officer), 38
Romilly sur Seine, 185
Roosevelt, Pres. Franklin D., 150
Roosevelt Hotel, New Orleans, La., 7
Royal Canadian Air Force, 47
Royal Dutch Shell Oil Company, 161

2nd Air Division, 58, 93, 114
17th Airborne Division, 185
Saalfield, Germany, 188
St. Brieux, France, 72
St. George Hotel, 35, 39, 41
St. Nazaire, France, 54, 74

St. Omer, France, 5, 7
Sarasota, Fla., 19
Schweinfurt, Germany, 82, 83, 97, 100
Sebring Army Air Field, 77
Sergeant, Capt. Roland, 84
Seward, Capt. "Eddie," 56
Sexton, Col. William T., 42
Sharingham, England, 66
Shell Oil, 161
Shilling, Col. David, 152, 155
Siegfried Line, 188
Sikeston, Mo., 10
Sindelfingen, Germany, 175
Singer Sewing Machine Company, 174
Smith, Maj. Gen. Bedell, 30, 38, 39
Smith, Col. Dale, 88, 162, 163
Smyrl, Lt. Col. James, 185–86
Southeast Training Command, 16
Spaatz, Gen. Carl A., 31, 35, 36, 37, 45, 47, 77, 150, 180
Spahnhoeck, Mr., 132, 133, 134
Spencer, Lt. Horace, 175, 176, 177, 180
Sperry, Lt., 102, 108
Spillman, S/Sgt. Leslie G., 176, 177
Spratt, S/Sgt. Jack, 175, 176, 177
Springfield, Mass., 20
Stalag Luft III, 67, 76
Stanbridge Earles, 123, 185, 186
Stars and Stripes, 68, 183
Steger, Lt. Floyd, 137
Stevenson, Capt. Mellor W., 161, 162, 163, 164, 165, 170
Stornoway, Scotland, 24
Strasbourg, France, 87
Strategic Air Command, 54
Stuttgart, Germany, 28

Summersby, Kay, 38, 39
Sutton, Col. James, 1, 2, 3, 4, 18, 52

3rd Air Force, 190
3rd Air Division, 54, 58, 83, 85, 94, 101, 114, 168
13th Combat Wing, 93
12th Tactical Air Force, 30, 150
301st Bomb Group, 1, 3, 37, 53
303rd Bomb Group, 53
305th Bomb Group, 53, 54, 55, 67, 68, 88, 110, 121, 121, 169, 170
306th Bomb Group, 53, 54, 55, 67, 68, 88, 110, 121, 169, 170
325th Bomb Squadron, 3, 68, 85, 112, 113, 188
326th Bomb Squadron, 22, 60, 114, 176
327th Bomb Squadron, 4, 60
369th Bomb Squadron, 70
382nd Bomb Group, 55, 124
384th Bomb Group, 88, 152, 163
390th Bomb Group, 93
Teaford, Edward E., 28, 43, 46
Telergma, Tunisa, 37
Texaco Oil Company, 65
Texas A&M University, 10, 11
Tippen, John W., 28
Todd, Maj. Wilson P., 113
Travis, Gen. Robert, 86, 88
Travis Air Force Base, 89
True, Lt. Donald, 54
True Magazine, 97
Tucher, Johnnie J., 28
Turner, Gen. Howard M., 109, 185
Twelve O'Clock High, 50, 68
Twinning, Gen. Nathan F., 150
Tyler, Texas, 16

United States Military Academy, 162, 169
United States Army Air Corps Instrument Flight School, 16
University of Arkansas, 10
Upton, Lt. K.S., 33, 40, 41
USO, 51

V-2, 156
Van der Lay, Dr., 138, 139, 140, 141, 142
Van Horne, S/Sgt. John, 105
Vorden, Holland, 132, 133, 134
Vor Runstedt, Gen., 184

Wahoo Mark II, 68
Walsh, S/Sgt. Joseph M., 65
Walton, S/Sgt. Reece B., 64
Ward, Capt. Frank, 56
Washington, D.C., 22
Washington & Lee University, 161, 162

Weaver, S/Sgt. Tyre C., 62, 65
Western Union Telegraph Company, 153
Westover Army Air Field, 19
West Virginia University, 8, 154
Wiley, Lt. Eugene, 4, 20
Williams, Capt. David, 124
Williams, Gen. Robert, 163, 164, 168, 170
Wilson, Lt. Gen. James W., 169, 170, 173, 174, 189
Winterswik, Holland, 129
Word, Maj. McGehee, 86, 87, 114, 115, 116, 166
Worth, Capt. Edgar, 156
Wright Field, Ohio, 54
Wyler, Maj. William, 49, 50, 61, 152

YB-40, 54, 55, 60, 112

Zemke, Col. Hubert, 59, 152